AMERICA According To Me

BERNIE COOK

Copyright © 2011 Bernie Cook

All rights reserved.

ISBN: 10: 1467917532
ISBN-13: 978-1467917537

'Twenty years from now you will be more disappointed by the things you didn't do than by the ones you did do. So throw off the bowlines, sail away from the safe harbor. Catch the trade winds in your sails. Explore. Dream. Discover.'

Mark Twain

ABOUT THE AUTHOR

Bernie Cook was born in New Zealand not far from the ends of the earth. As soon as he thought he was grown up, he was determined to find out for himself if the rest of the world actually existed or was just a marketing ploy of advertisers.

Over the next 30 years, he traveled almost everywhere and at last has the courage to tell rest of the world what he found.

Today he lives at the beach near Auckland, not far from the start of the earth

BERNIE COOK

CONTENTS

	Prelude	9
1	The South	12
2	The Seat of Power	23
3	A New York Minute	29
4	RVing Around America	41
5	Wedding, The First	44
6	Bikers On The Move	50
7	Yellowstone	58
8	Officials of the United States	68
9	A Nasty Encounter	80
10	Salt Lake City	87
11	Sin City	90
12	California Dreaming	114
13	Wedding, The Second	121
14	Dances With Sharks	126
15	Home	132

PRELUDE

I have learned, as a New Zealander newly arrived in the United States, that when travelling in America, to greet and compliment another driver, you honk your horn, raise your arm out the window in a closed hand salute and shout 'Ass hoooole!!' To which I've also learned the correct response is to make a letter 'L' with your thumb and index finger, wave it at them and yell back; 'I've got a gun!'

At least that's what seemed to be the case in the seedier parts of Miami, Florida where our Great American Road Trip began. Naturally, after encountering such behaviors, reasonable but inexperienced travelers might think they would be prevalent throughout the 48 contiguous states and naturally they would be wrong.

Generalizations can be such fun but do little credit to others who can and do behave quite differently to each other according to their race, beliefs, region, state or level of education in this huge, diverse land.

What the rest of the world sees as a monolithic and homogenous super power is in fact an iron-tight union of 50 quite different countries, populated across its many borders by people of every race and creed on Earth. A gigantic stew pot of ethnicities with their own cultures that overlap and interact but don't necessarily mix into a great melting pot as some would have us believe.

Overlaying the lot however, is a system of government and a sense of national unity despite the differences, that has given rise to the most powerful and influential society the world has ever seen.

A study of contemporary American culture from the point of view of a road traveler in a Recreational Vehicle or RV can provide a fascinating insight to the lives of ordinary Americans in different regions and states outside the main cities. Our method of study was simply to travel in a general direction along routes off the main highways, dropping into towns as required for supplies, rest and relaxation and whatever else came along the way including unplanned vehicle repairs and doctors visits, and interact with the locals. The ordinary Americans we met living their daily lives, were as different to each other as it is possible to get, but all were interesting to us as amateur anthropologists keen to sample what America was all about.

The trouble with touring America by road is that it is huge. I mean really, really big. It's easy to calculate the distances on a map and estimate the driving times, but when you actually have to do it, the immensity of the place begins to dawn on you.

When you see thousands of cars and trucks of all sizes on the freeways coming and going, entering and leaving continuously both ways at a near uniform speed that ridicules the driving skills of the average motorist elsewhere; when you realize that the area you have travelled in for the last four hours is a minor part of a small state in the South; when a high rise city whose name you have never heard of before rises majestically out of the endless expanse of trees as you travel and you realize that this pattern is being repeated a hundred times in just the east coast of the United States simultaneously, then you begin to understand how vast and developed is this amazing country.

A road trip by RV that started in Miami, Florida, went through 25 states and ended in San Diego, California covering some 12,000 kilometers, is a big undertaking by most people's standards. Especially if you're not completely sure the RV you bought on Ebay actually exists or the guy will really pick you up from the airport as he said he would.

Coming from a country where you drive on the left hand side of the road presented a further challenge although my ability to drive on the right hand side was obviously of an unexpectedly high standard given the number of greetings and compliments described earlier that I received, even within the first few minutes of my getting behind the wheel.

This light-hearted look at our personal encounters will hopefully amuse, entertain and inform you. I do not claim this to be a definitive examination of the American Way, just my observations seen through slightly mad eyes and which must be taken with a pinch of salt here and there, but overall, it is a reflection of me and my wife's experiences plus reactions to the people we met and the things we did.

1. THE SOUTH

Miami is where we started our great road journey and is about as far south as you can go in the United States without actually arriving in Cuba, although we could be forgiven for thinking we had crossed a border somewhere along the way as the primary spoken language seems to be Spanish with many of the locals claiming a link with Cuba. I almost felt like a foreigner. Even people who are obviously not of Latino origin speak Spanish before English in shopping centers and the like.

However it was a chance for me to practice that Spanish I had been working on for decades, so when it came time for ordering at the restaurant I was able to say, 'hey amigo, soy una puta y me gustaría hablar con las albóndigas por favor' or something like that which left my waiter and everyone around me in stitches.

'What?' I demanded indignantly.

'You just said you were a whore wanting to speak to the meatballs,' my host explained, between gales of laughter.

Needless to say that was the last time I attempted Spanish until I could be sure I was in a place where there was no one around who could understand it. That place turned out to be Cesspit, Tennessee where they were also having trouble with English and the married couples looked like brothers and sisters.

The food of America is as varied as its people. We had the opportunity to sample the delights of Cuban food whilst in Miami. Our Cuban-American host ordered for us and two Cuban Steaks the size of a small Asian country were served. Not surprising then is that the place was full of Spanish speaking people who themselves were each the size of several small Asians.

All this struck me as a little odd and out of place since our host had proudly announced that he was taking us to an Australian restaurant obviously believing that this was a compliment and a treat for New Zealanders. Overlooking the nationalist slight that the average American would probably be unaware of, I resigned myself to the joys of eating Australian fare that in Australia can be really good but in Florida might be something quite different.

I was pleasantly surprised to discover that apart from a couple of plastic boomerangs stuck to the wall, a picture or two of kangaroos and the name of the restaurant, it bore no resemblance to Australian cuisine or anything Australian for that matter. It was firmly an American style restaurant providing American style food with a Cuban flavor. The service was great, the food was wonderful, the wine expensive and the company congenial so we marked the occasion as a success.

Eager to get moving the next day, we provisioned the RV which, to my relief was real and as described by our Ebay vendor, and headed for the beach which unfortunately turned out to be owned by someone else. We were able to get within a stone's throw of the shore according to the GPS, but our way was barred by a continuous row of hotels, resorts and private homes that seemed to run right down to the sea and through which we were not allowed to venture.

A small shark-infested beach about the size of a hotel foyer had been set aside for the poor people, but all three parking spaces were full and it looked like a gun fight was about to get underway between rival drug gangs on the shore so we left Miami and headed north where I was sure we would find real America.

That evening we stayed at a nearly deserted and very run-down campground at Cape Canaveral. The owners were nowhere to be seen and there was no one to collect the money. We chose a site for the RV and set up camp anyway expecting that someone would venture along at some time. Taking a walk around the grounds, we finally met an English speaking American who turned out to be polite and shy. 'This must be what real America is all about.' I thought to myself. She lived permanently in her rented caravan and was demure and shy when we spoke to her. She must have been quite ill in fact as she was self-administering some intravenous medication and was too busy to talk much.

Another resident in a string vest sitting on a beer crate outside his caravan complimented me when I spoke to him as I walked past which I thought was odd since I wasn't driving. I gave him the 'L' sign and he disappeared quickly into his caravan.

It occurred to me that we should secure all doors and windows despite the heat and sleep with one eye open with a heavy object near to hand. Just in case.

The air conditioning in the RV was a blessing in the oppressive heat that was to dog us right up the east coast in a heat wave that had the popular media predicting Doomsday and expert talking heads rubbing their hands in glee at what they saw was incontrovertible evidence of Global Warming.

The night passed without incident and we headed north in the morning.

The Kennedy Space Center is a theme park dedicated to the display and sale of the fast food which is in abundant supply right around America. Much of the food is served in buckets similar in size to those used in European piggeries. The idea being, I believe, to eat as much as you can then try to squeeze yourself through tubes and capsules that look a little like rockets. Many of the locals had obviously graduated to the point where the tubes and capsules were insufficient to accommodate their generous dimensions. Many of these had apparently gone on to become guides and were able to tell the rest of us where to queue or which way to walk to find a supply of buckets.

There are apparently no more all-you-can-eat restaurants in America any longer due to people being able to eat several buckets full each thus destroying the business model.

We soon left Florida behind and headed inland through Georgia in the hope of escaping the heat wave. We may as well have entered a completely new country, so different it was to Florida.

This then was the real South, which is the home of fundamental Christians. The so called Bible Belt. Every small town we passed through had Christian churches of all denominations known to God plus a few I had never heard of including the Church of Transformation Episcopal, Full Gospel Revival, Redeemed Freewill Baptist, Daper Valley Pentecostal Holiness Church, Ebeneza Church of the Exalted Few and the Chapel Of The Patron Saint of Rednecks.

While we saw plenty of Christian Churches, we didn't see any Christians, it being Tuesday. On Sundays when they are out in fervent force and after the pastors and ministers have completed their bell ringing competition, the believers sing gospel songs loud enough so the wrong thinkers in the church down the road can hear them and get really pissed off which causes them in turn to sing really loud as well. The effect is an otherwise pleasant, green countryside reverberating with the disturbing sound of discordant hymns that never made the Top 40 five hundred years ago and could quite possibly be the reason Christ has never kept his promise to return.

The one thing they can agree on however is the right to bear arms. A bumper sticker we saw said it all: 'I believe in gun control. You need two hands to keep it steady'. Guns and Christ. What could be more natural? I believe the time is now right to establish the Church of Guns For Christ whose motto could be: 'Shoot Thy Neighbor before He Shooteth You'.

The rest of the week they play country music on the radio, the twangy, whiny, 'I lost my horse' kind of stuff. This is interspersed with discourse from expert talking heads who sound like an irate Jed Clampett from the Beverly Hillbillies on how the Muslim devil in the form of Barrack Obama is destroying the country and their Christian Way Of Life. I asked a checkout operator at a local Wal-Mart who wanted God to bless me when I paid for the goods, if she knew what happened if you played country music backwards. Of course she had no idea either what happened when you did that or what I was talking about. That was not enough reason for me not to continue as anyone who knows me would know, so I told her that you got your job back, your wife came back to you and your dog came back to life. She looked at me for a moment, pressed her intercom button and called the resident Texan to aisle 7 immediately. I gave her the 'L' sign and left as the flashing lights and howling sirens rocketed down the road.

Speaking of Texans.

I was lucky enough to encounter one at an Auto Parts Supply shop in South Carolina. This is not as difficult as it may appear at first glance since we have had to stop at every Auto Parts Supply shop in the South in a thus far successful effort to keep the RV going, so we were destined to meet one sooner or later.

Whilst trying to work out why a light bulb he was selling wouldn't fit my RV, the discussion turned to the current heat wave which naturally lead to my new friend saying that he had just gotten out of the Marine Corps and that this was not hot compared to where he had been.

'Have you been in Iraq?' I queried. Indeed he had and had enjoyed every minute of it and was mightily pissed that he wasn't still there.

'Why didn't you re-enlist?' I offered. He had tried but Barrack Obama was down-sizing the military and they didn't want him.

'Did you shoot any rag heads?' I ventured.

'Sure, plenty,' was his nonchalant reply. That's why he loved it and wanted to go back. There were some left. None of this dear horrified Reader, is exaggerated for literary effect. This is exactly how the discussion took place. I then asked him if he was a true Southern Christian and he gave me the 'L' sign and I disappeared quickly into my RV. Needless to say I still needed a bulb for the RV.

Texas was removed from our itinerary.

Christianity is alive and well in North Carolina too. The blessing business is big here. God is surely busy carrying out the blessings requested of him from everyone we meet. I'm not sure which way to take this. Either I am rising to a saintly status as a result of the blessings raining down upon me or they have noted that I need a great deal of forgiveness if I am ever to get to heaven myself.

Trying to find a campground around dusk along the Blue Ridge Parkway in North Carolina can be difficult given the winding country roads and impenetrable forest that reaches to the very edge of the road. However one was found and a delightful lady, who spoke Clampettish English, called me sir, organized a site for the RV and begged God to bless me when I paid her even though we were $3 short of the amount she wanted. With no method of receiving payment available at their office other than cash, I promised to back track 147 miles to the nearest ATM to get her the $3 by morning.

'That will not be a problem Sir,' she demurred. She looked forward to receiving the $3 when I was ready and May God Bless Me.

In an earlier encounter in a town further south we had not only been bestowed with a God Bless You Sir by a sweet old lady at the Laundromat who looked like everyone's aunty, but also gifted with a great box of sour blackberries which we could turn into jam if only we had 3 ton of sugar, a 400 gallon vat, a ladle the size of a small tree and a furnace.

Having transported the consignment of blackberries 400 miles with no sign of a spare vat along the way, and not knowing where we were going to sleep due to the blackberries occupying the entire bed, inspiration suddenly struck me.

'Would you like these delicious blackberries in exchange for the $3 we owe you?' I asked cunningly.

'Ya'll would have to ask mah husband,' she smiled sweetly. 'He's over theah drinkin' moonshine with the campers by the barbeque.'

I wandered over to the group of men swaying gently in the still air.

'Are you Cletus?' I asked the dude with the bandana wrapped around his head and a pony tail hanging down his back.

'Depends,' he replied, 'whether Ah owe you money or you owe me.'

'Ah owe you $3,' I countered slipping into his accent just because it seemed cool to do so.

'Innat case Ah'll just go get mah gun,' he said nonchalantly, turning away from me.

'Don't bother man,' I rejoined. 'When you're big enough to take me, you'll be too old. And too slow.'

He seemed to like this and agreed to settle the debt for the mountain of sour blackberries. No doubt they would end up in the still and be offered up as moonshine to next lot of campers.

Suspicious looking clear liquid with a strong top up of Coke was proffered to me in a plastic cup. A drip onto the paint work of the barbeque table resulted worryingly in an instant blister and a small vent of steam.

'Where ya'll from?' he inquired.

'New Zealand,' I replied.

'Grunt,' he said.

'You know where that is?' I challenged.

'Hell no, an' Ah don't care.'

'C'mon,' I encouraged, 'have a guess.'

'Somewhere near Newfoundland?' he ventured. 'Hell Ah've only bin to two states, Louisiana an' here,' he boasted, looking at me like I had just landed from Mars.

'New Zealand is near Australia,' I grumped, giving up.

'Had an Australian here once, but never had a Noo Zealander.' He mused. 'Don't know that I want another one neither.'

That comment marked the high point for the witticisms as the strange liquid slowly took hold of us both and the conversation deteriorated to an even lower intellectual level.

I awoke at 4am on my back beside the barbeque not recognizing the spinning stars in the northern sky and with insects gnawing away at my bare skin. Cletus was nowhere to be seen and the blackberries had disappeared along with the moonshine.

My other companion at the barbeque party that night was a high school teacher from Florida on his usual vacation to the same campground each year. Unlike Cletus, he knew all about New Zealand and raved about what a beautiful place it was even though he had never been there but wanted to go one day. It transpired that we were to hear the same story from Americans everywhere who were basing their views on Peter Jackson's Lord Of The Rings movies which showed magnificent natural scenery that they could apparently get to by a short taxi ride from Auckland International Airport and be back for lunch. I didn't have the heart to tell them that much of it was computer generated graphics for which several Oscars were awarded and I figured the country could use the overseas funds if only half of them turned up, so I said nothing.

'If only it didn't take three days on a plane to get there.' They would moan. I would try to explain that the flight was 12 hours not 3 days and that crossing the International Dateline sent them hurtling into the future. This simply didn't register with them as making any sense but cracking a time travelling joke was simply too hard to resist.

'But don't worry, when you come back, you will travel back to your own time and regain the lost day. In fact you will be in Los Angeles before you leave Auckland, which is kinda handy because if the plane crashes, you just don't get on it.'

This logic was too much for most of them and an International Dateline sounded suspiciously like a dating service of European origin crossed with a time travelling episode of Star Trek. I would be rewarded with a long, strange stare along with a muttered explanation that there were things they needed to attend to.

No doubt the thought of meeting more strange New Zealanders put them off the trip despite the lure of the Lord Of The Rings.

With the effects of Louisiana moonshine pounding in my head, we set off in the morning for the Blue Ridge Parkway which had been touted by all and sundry in the South as a 'must see'. Not really knowing what a Parkway might be but suspecting it could be a little like the Southern Motorway in Auckland at misnamed 'rush hour', when the cars are basically parked, we got on it to discover that it was a limited access road for cars and RVs only (I think RVs were allowed) that went through a forest park. There. Solved.

It stretched nearly 500 miles through 3 states along the Appalachian Mountain chain and was just two lanes of opposing traffic, the lanes being slightly narrower than the RV. While there was little opposing traffic, what did pass us was so close that my nerves were shattered after just a few miles as cars whistled past with just inches to spare. What the drivers of the cars were thinking as a monstrous RV taking up half of their lane thundered towards them with its driver ashen-faced and wrestling with the steering wheel is anyone's guess, but it could be a good bet that bowels might have loosened a little. While I might walk 500 Miles to fall down at your door, there was no way I was going to squeeze an RV 500 Miles down that Long and Winding Road so we got off and took The Long Way Home.

2. THE SEAT OF POWER

Washington DC is not a state but a District carved out of the states of Maryland and Virginia in 1800 to be the capital of the new republic. The position was chosen for its central location between the northern and southern states in the hope that neither party would be insulted and wage war over it. It is the new Rome of the 21st Century. The centre of the Earth as far as the wielding of power goes, and it attracts those who like to wield power like flies to honey. Along with that come those who don't like those who wield the power. In other words it is a magnet for the powerful and the powerless. That in turn leads to the fourth arm of Government, Security, since powerless Americans have a habit of shooting their powerful Presidents.

The other group of people who are attracted to this power and its subsequent display in its grand buildings, memorials, totem poles and parks are tourists who come to gawk at it all and hope to catch a glimpse of the powerful, which they don't because of all the security. The powerless on the other hand are in evidence with their protests which seem to be a daily occurrence on the streets around the White House. They don't see the powerful either.

Security has now become part of the pomp and ceremony of the Republic. It allows those who conduct it to become somewhat powerful themselves. The hunt for terrorists seems to be a boring occupation, judging from the demeanor of the guards, since none are ever found among the thousands of thronging, sweating tourists pushing and crowding their way into the visitors centres of the White House and Capitol, which have been set up to keep them away from the real buildings. Museums and other public buildings also feature security consisting of bag inspections, metal detectors and x-ray machines pretty much the same as for airports.

The difference between this new Rome and the old Rome is that while both are jammed with tourists and the people who feed off them, in Washington the tourists are tolerated rather than welcomed. The power of old Rome has long since evaporated leaving the shell to be admired and wondered at. The power of Washington however, is real and only just hidden behind the impenetrable walls protecting the seat of power. Yet it is the tourists who occupy Washington with the mighty concealing themselves out of sight in their pocket fortresses. Look but don't get too close is the message and while the lookers are looking, the every-present secret service is looking back and making no effort to be secret about it. There is even a uniformed branch of the Secret Service that has logo-plastered cars. The irony of the contradiction seems to have escaped those responsible.

Being somewhat powerful myself in terms of being able to zoom my camera lens through the bars of the fence, across the vast expanse of the White House front lawn, (the Obamas have most of their fun on the back lawn apparently) and to the roof of the White House where I observed a massive man clad in black with his trousers tucked menacingly into his socks. He was silhouetted against a perfect blue sky which was just visible through the smog and looking back at me through equally powerful binoculars. He also had what appeared to be a snipers rifle on a tripod. I felt reasonably on par with him in terms of power due to the distance between us until my wife asked me what the wavering red dot on my forehead was.

Given he was dressed in black from head to toe in 40 degree heat and in direct sunlight reflecting off a very White building, I decided that he might not be enjoying his job all that much and rather than antagonize him further, sought refuge in the air conditioned White House Visitor's Center two blocks away where I was able to study small models of the White House rooms. I thought closer examination of the model might reveal small figurines looking like the Obamas frozen in place dealing competently and efficiently with a world crisis, but either they had been placed in a model of a local burger restaurant to represent Presidential Date Night or there weren't any at all. My sense of power was further diminished when, upon entering the building, my bag was examined in detail with a stick by a short, very stout woman who clearly did not like me or her job. Scowling at me because I hadn't placed my bag exactly in front of her, thus forcing her to gesture impatiently at me to move it half an inch closer, she opened the bag with a gloved hand and pushed her stick deep within. She was obviously not too concerned about a bomb suddenly going off in her face, but judging from the distasteful expression while she poked through my bag with her stick, she expected to find bodily fluids or any number of revolting and possible contagious things that might adhere to her stick or get on her clothing. After much prodding, poking and peering, the bag was certified non-lethal and sent through the checkpoint leaving me with a disquieting sense of personal violation. I was then required to walk through the x-ray door which of course erupted in a howl of noise causing heads to turn and pop up everywhere like meercats looking for leopards.

'Step this way Sir,' required the enormous black guard dressed like a Nazi SS Officer advancing on me and holding a huge, vicious looking rod that I hoped wasn't an enema.

'Can you show me that step again, I missed it the first time but anyway, I don't dance so good. Got no rhythm,' I teased.

They either hire people with no sense of humor, the stultifying boring nature of their job drives it right out of them after the first week or - unlikely as it may seem - my joke wasn't funny. Whichever way it was, my attempt at humor to brighten the day for everyone fell on deaf ears. After running his rod all over my body I was certified acceptable to enter the building. It left me wondering why, after all the false alarms generated by x-ray machines, they don't build them out of the rod scanners, which are apparently definitive, in the first place.

A highlight of our trip to Washington was visiting the enormous memorial to the soldiers who died in WWII. It is a magnificent memorial which not only honors those who died but also boasts of glorious victories against the Germans and Japanese. I commented to my wife that German and Japanese tourists would probably not like it. As fate would have it, there was a couple on our tour bus who failed to rendezvous with the bus at the end of this stage of the tour since they didn't go to the memorial. When they finally rejoined us, I noted with some amusement that he was Japanese and she was German.

It was our turn at the next stop to be left without a bus. We left a museum at the wrong end and missed the bus that was waiting for us at the front. By the time the error dawned on us, it was too late, the bus had gone. With panic and stress setting in we decided to get a taxi to the last rendezvous point so we could at least get back to our RV. My wife hailed a cab at exactly the same time as I spotted our bus driving slowly down the road. Washington was brought to sudden halt as I attempted to run down the bus in the middle of the road while she threw herself in front of the cab to force it to stop. Pandemonium ensued as all traffic came to a stop as we were both successful in halting our respective vehicles at the same time.

'I've found our bus!' I screamed as the wife yelled that she had found a cab. Washington is not stopped by anyone for long and in a moment the traffic was hurtling by her giving her compliments by the dozen as she dodged and darted her way through 6 lanes of thundering, traffic.

To our astonishment, the bus was empty apart from Bob the driver.

'It's a good thing you're a great tipper,' he said. 'I came back for you.' This left me with the uneasy feeling that I had not yet fully understood the American system of tipping and might have paid too much in our time there. He then took us to the Ford Theatre to catch up with the rest. Ironically, possibly due to our being late, we were not scrutinized by security. It almost seemed a waste that I did not have a bomb or a gun. We followed in the path of John Wilkes Booth, who shot Abraham Lincoln in that very theatre, up the stairs and around the back of the audience to the booth in which Lincoln had been. (No pun intended there, but I'll take it.) Like then, the place was packed and like him, we were late arriving for the show which was well underway. Unlike him, everyone noticed our entrance. The show we saw was in fact a history lesson on that incident.

We learned Booth chose a moment in the play to shoot when everyone would laugh at a witty line thus concealing his shot. That he then jumped from the booth to the stage did nothing to enhance his plan of getting away without being noticed although most of the audience apparently thought it was part of the show. We were given the witty line and no one laughed. Our hostess assured us that we were not alone. None of her audiences laughed. This was due, she reasoned, to changes in society and the line was no longer funny. Perhaps her delivery needed a little work or a President getting shot to death is just not funny.

We learned that after the shooting, Lincoln was carried across the street to a house and put in the owner's bed where he died the next day. Small but vital details in the tale such as the fact that Lincoln was so tall his feet poked over the end of the bed were thankfully not omitted. We declined the opportunity to stand in the boiling sun for 20 minutes waiting for our turn to see the very bed in which he died.

We had a beer instead at the air conditioned Hard Rock Cafe down the road and pondered the different direction history must have taken.

Apparently nothing in America is too tragic that it can't be turned into a tourist opportunity. How long before we see guided tours of Ground Zero?

While the Kennedy Space Center is a theme park, the Smithsonian in Washington is the real deal. We saw the actual capsules that returned from the moon along with earlier space craft. Informative, fascinating and genuinely historic, the Aerospace building could have kept me enthralled all day however we had just an hour to soak up as much as we could. It deserves a return visit. The other five Smithsonian buildings housed much different exhibits and no doubt a week could be spent exploring them all.

3. A NEW YORK MINUTE

New York is the greatest city on Earth. So say those who live there. It's hard to argue with them as the city is indeed great, vast, culturally diverse and magnificent. On a previous visit to New York, we discovered that New Yorkers were kind, friendly and helpful. This was expected to be the case again this time.

Manhattan is an island covered in a lot of very tall buildings and which was once Native American, then Dutch, then English, then American, then English again and finally back to American as a result of everyone wanting to live there and prepared to have a fight over it. We were taken to the downtown area of Canal Street in Manhattan by our kind, friendly and helpful hosts who lived across the border in New Jersey, although it is difficult to know just when you are arriving in which city since the urban area seems continuous from Washington through to Boston. However the locals seem know where they are and without a fight are able to sneak into Manhattan through cleverly concealed tunnels controlled by guards who are easily bribed with a few dollars.

Being America of course, these tunnels are large enough to take your car comfortably so you don't have to do any crawling and mess up your hair. (According to rumor, an escape from a Nazi Prisoner of War camp in WWII was stymied because the British wanted a simple tunnel that got them into the woods where they could make their getaway and the Americans wanted a four lane, air conditioned tunnel that emerged in Trafalgar Square. By the time they had worked through all the procedures with the British insisting on protocol being observed, the war was over and they walked out the gate.)

We sneaked easily into Manhattan via one of the tunnels and

found a park on the street. Real estate is in great demand in Manhattan, particularly places to park your car and these can be fought over to the death. Inches count. No sooner had we alighted from our car, than we were accosted by the very excitable father and teenage son (so they claimed to be) who owned the car in front. We had not left enough room for them get out according to their incorrect version of the facts.

'Are you crazy?' inquired our host? 'I could drive a truck outta there.'

Within seconds the debate had descended into a verbal screaming match with arms waving and lots of jumping around. This seemed to be the ideal opportunity for me to start my video camera. The precocious 17 year old brat claiming to be the son of the driver, then wanted me arrested for filming a minor which apparently proved beyond doubt that I was a paedophile. He whipped out his cell phone to record this hideous act and we faced each other in the street like a pair of Old Western gun fighters.

The shooting commenced.

'I got you, I got you!' he screamed. 'You're going to jail.'

Not being aware of the rules of this particular rite, I kept shooting while he danced around like Michael Jackson on speed. It occurred to me that I was getting better footage than he was and I mentally calculated the hits on You Tube I would get when it went viral.

Meanwhile dad, or his client, depending on your suspicions, had dialled 911 to summon the police. With his faced twisted in a rictus of rage, he advised our host that he would get what was coming to him and if lucky, would spend the rest of his miserable live rotting in Leavenworth, although he believed the death sentence was appropriate in this case and would be pushing for it.

The police seemed to take a long time to arrive which is strange because in New York there are more police than people.

Meanwhile the posturing and threats continued and eventually a better park for our host's car became available over the road, so the car was moved there.

This was extremely disappointing for the complainant as he could no longer show the police he was trapped. Bravely he decided to wait for the police anyway as he had a really good story to tell.

Finally a police car showed up and our tormentors miraculously developed a calm and reasonable demeanor they had hitherto failed to demonstrate. In tried and true police procedure, the two officers split up to get both sides of the story. Their quest appeared to be aided by the mysterious occupants of a non-descript, brown GM car sitting in a vacant section across the road and which had been there the whole time. Like all non-descript, brown GM cars, it was clearly an undercover cop car with two undercover cops trying desperately to blend in with the rest of the population. Someone needs to explain to the bureaucrats who pay for these things that having a non-descript, brown GM car with no fancy hub caps or other form of pimping is a dead giveaway, especially in New York City. It seemed to be recognised instantly as such by one of the officers who wandered over to the car to get a report from the occupants who had witnessed the whole sorry episode and at the same time, blowing their cover for whatever stakeout or lunch break they were on. After receiving a full report from the mysterious witnesses, the officer returned to the scene of the crime apparently satisfied that she had solved the case beyond a reasonable doubt and compared notes with her partner who had drawn the short straw and dealt with the protagonists. Justice is swift on the streets of New York City as it was only moments before they came to their conclusion and to the great disappointment of the complainant, our host did not receive an immediate death sentence but was instead rewarded with a handshake from the officer who appeared less than impressed with the complaint.

The charge of me being a lurking paedophile interested in filming a skinny white, ranting idiot remains untested in Court to this day. I remain on the run but I don't think anyone is looking for me.

Interestingly they claimed not to be New Yorkers but New Jersyians, so my fantasy of New Yorkers being kind, friendly and helpful remains intact for now. About then I noticed a peculiar looking appendage attached to the man's chest. A closer look revealed a small, pathetic dog housed in some form of harness.

'You're wearing a dog.' I commented. 'Why are you wearing a dog?'

He stared at me with mad eyes for a moment and I made a mental note not to antagonize unhinged people.

The next act for the New York Street Show we seemed to have stumbled upon appeared immediately. Three fire engines and a Fire Chief vehicle wailed and flashed their way into the tight streets and stopped behind us blocking off access to the intersection.

Out of them poured New York's finest Fire Fighters in full fire fighting regalia.

There followed an intense period of investigation of a fence around a construction site on the intersection. The police car blocked one street while the officers filed their report seemingly oblivious to the excitement nearby, the fire appliances blocked two others and our by now humbled and silent complainants blocked the last street as they tried to get away from it all. Radios crackled through the alleys and I fully expected to see Bruce Willis hurtling through on a horse to save the day. A discrete inquiry with one of the fire fighters and with my Action Cam in hand still rolling, revealed the full scope of the emergency. To my disappointment it was nothing more than the fence was about to fall over. The tension was palpable as they inspected the fence in order of rank whilst the multi-colored emergency lights on the vehicles flashed around and off the buildings. After several riveting minutes a decision was reached. One of them gave it kick and it fell over.

Then they went home.

After thanking our host for the morning's entertainment and expressing our amazement at how well he seemed to have organized our New York Minute for us, we then proceeded on foot to our original destination in the next street.

Great bargains are to be had in Canal St, New York. Friendly, helpful and kind African American men on the street picked me out of the crowd to offer me a wonderful Rolex watch for just $120. I was much impressed and honored that I had been chosen for this kind gesture. Modestly refusing to take advantage of the gentleman, I declined but he proved once again how generous New Yorkers can be by lowering the price to $40 despite my protests.

Now I'm smart enough to know that a Rolex watch is worth a lot more than that, so greed overcame me.

'I'll need to take a look at it first' I said. With that, he glanced nervously around and gestured me closer.

'Here,' he said revealing a gleaming gold watch inside his

jacket pocket. 'Don't let anyone see.' He muttered in my ear conspiratorially. 'Take it into the shop. But don't let anyone see you.' The watch slid smoothly out of his pocket and, concealed in his hand, slipped it quickly into mine all the while his eyes were darting up and down the street. I stepped inside the shop doorway as instructed and opened my hand to inspect my prize. 'Man! Don't show everyone!' he hissed. I quickly closed my fist and affected a nonchalant air while trying to peek surreptitiously at the watch. I could only assume that he had taken a real liking to me and didn't want anyone else to have this wonderful bargain. I was puzzled by the expression on the face of the store owner whose store I was in. It seemed he was unhappy about something and advanced toward me with a glare. 'Get outta there man!' my new friend advised me and guided me back out onto the street where we were soon lost in the throng of people moving past.

'Is it automatic or do I have to wind it up every day?' I asked.

'Huh? Man it's automatic. Gimme the money!' he demanded. He seemed to be getting more and more nervous with beads of sweat breaking out on his forehead.

'Does is it come with a warranty?' I asked.

'Yeah, yeah, whatever man, if it breaks I'll send you a new one.' He responded. Suddenly another African American gentleman a few yards away in the crowd yelled,

'Yo, Leon, muthafukka!' By chance it turned out that my new friend's name was Leon as well and he was obviously not feeling all that great suddenly as he seemed to have turned a little pale.

'Hurry up man!' he implored me so I gave him $40 and watched him vanish quickly into the crowd with his other friend pushing through the throng towards him.

'That bloke must've wanted the watch himself for that price. Too bad. You snooze, you lose' I thought to myself smugly.

Such a nice chap.

There proved to be many more generous and kind African American men just like him down the street and I was overcome by the offers of ludicrously undervalued Rolex watches.

The next day we tried to sneak back through the tunnels into Manhattan in our RV without the protection of our hosts, however the guards could not be bribed on this occasion and we were turned away on account of our vehicle having some sort of substance aboard that might blow up the tunnel. BBQ gas was apparently listed as a weapon of mass destruction.

That left us to sneak across the only bridge we could find. I had to bribe the guard $11, but he didn't ask me about my gas so I didn't tell him.

New York City is full of cops. They can be found almost anywhere but usually standing in pairs in shop doorways. Unlike police from other parts of the world I've been to, two cheerful officers a male and female, seemed quite genial when I dared to take a quick look. Encouraged by the lack of any threatening looks from them that one might expect from police in other countries, I stopped to inspect them a little closer taking in the array of armaments each carried on their person. Along with a gun, a billy club, a Taser and an array of communication equipment, they also seemed to be carrying spray cans presumably for subduing minor threats that didn't require bullets such as flies, mosquitoes and street performers.

"Can I get a photo with New York's Finest?" I asked.

"Sure" was the response, "why don't I take one of you both

with my partner?" suggested the female cop.

"I'd prefer one with both of you if that's OK" to which she agreed so I handed the camera to my wife and grabbed a cop under each arm.

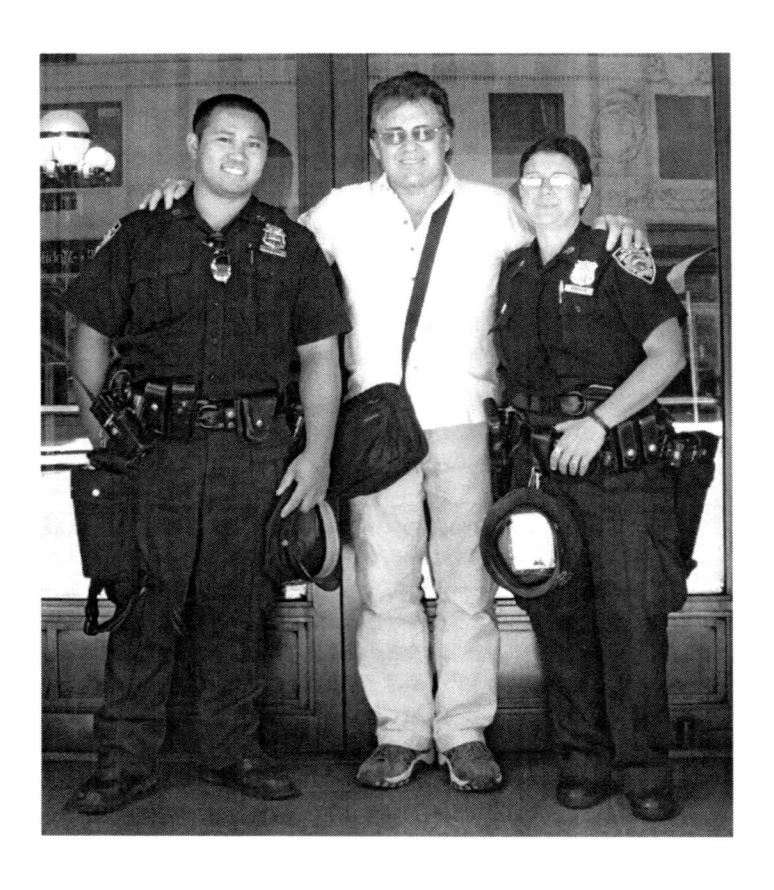

In any other place on Earth, this would result in instant arrest and probably a beating back in the cells, but these two were happy to oblige and saw no need to establish their authority. I was impressed and thought how much more effective they must be at their job and how much more cooperation they must get from the general public.

An exception to this rule is outside the Tower of London in England where the archaically dressed guards must stand rigid and unmoving at all times despite the atrocities committed on them by drunk Australian yobbos looking for a giggle. Oh how they must wish they could unleash their firepower on these imbeciles but the consequences of moving are obviously greater than the humiliation being visited upon them. Look closely however and you will observe that they are allowed to move their eyes and in this manner you can see the frustration and rage building, provided you're not blind drunk trying impress your mates. They quite clearly say that when they get off duty and out of their uniform they will hunt you down like the dog you are at whatever sleazy pub you are hanging out in, drag you by the hair into the street and kick the living shit out of you.

Londoners know that it is time to go home after a night out when they see Australians lying in the gutters.

Not so friendly as our New York cops were the security guards employed by the United Nations the headquarters of which are on Manhattan Island and not a part of the United States.

A visit to the headquarters showed the organization to be somewhat lacking in funds judging from the worn-out quality of the fit-out and the general air of malaise.

How effective it is at doing the job it was set up to do is a matter for debate, but the guards at the main entrance seemed determined to do their bit by refusing me permission to take their photograph on the way out. Apparently this would somehow compromise the ability of the United Nations to keep World Peace. No amount of cajoling seemed to work on these two who stood just inside United

Nation's territory.

"What will you do if I take a photo anyway?" I challenged.

"We will arrest you," was the reply.

"Really? What would I be charged with?"

They didn't seem to have an answer for that and it occurred to me that this is how authority in much of the world carries on, especially in countries that are less than democratic, so in that respect I guess the UN was being representative of its membership through its security guards.

Slightly riled at their attitude, I posed a solution:

"What if I step through these gates back into the United States and take a photo from there as I am entitled to do in a public area of a free country?"

"You are not permitted to take photographs" they insisted. Having already taken many photos including inside the General Assembly and Security Council without objection, I felt I needed to do my duty in the fight against tyranny and autocracy.

So in one graceful movement I boldly stepped back into the United States, turned, drew my camera and shot him.

As is so often the case when unreasonable authority's bluff is called, they did nothing other than grin impotently, the charade of their presumed power exposed.

I was happy to be back in the United States of America. The atmosphere was quite different.

Driving your RV through Manhattan is a wonderful thing. I thought it would be quite difficult but people were so helpful and friendly. Every time I changed lanes or changed my mind about which way to turn, they would give me a long friendly toot to let me know it was alright for me to squeeze our big, wide and tall RV in front of their small, dent-free car. Especially near Times Square. One even got up on the foot path to make room for us. A symphony of horns warmly accompanied us from one end of Manhattan to the other. We could have stayed all day. In fact we did because they wouldn't let us back through the tunnels to leave so we had to go back the way we came. But first we had to locate a particular store that proved to be the only one in North America that stocked the item we needed. The address given was on Broadway so we cruised slowly along the street looking for a park large enough to take the RV. As luck would have it I found one just a few yards from the store. Once again traffic came to a standstill while I maneuvered the giant RV into the park and once again, helpfully, I was guided by the horns of the friendly locals who were also happy to wave their arms about and shout encouragement for my efforts.

After getting what we came for and having a quick afternoon tea in the RV it was time to leave.

It seems that New Yorkers couldn't get enough of us as they waved and tooted all the way back to the mainland.

4. RVing AROUND AMERICA

The monstrous RV, barely inches away, thundered slowly alongside us on the freeway like the opening scene from Star Wars. Like a great Death Star it rumbled by inch by thundering inch. Caught in its vortex our tiny 25 foot RV swayed in the buffeting winds like we were trapped in a tractor beam. Wrestling grimly with the steering wheel, with beads of sweat forming on my brow, I tried desperately to hold the line in my lane and to keep from either hitting the side of the massive beast or plunging a 1,000 feet to our deaths from the bridge we were crossing. I needn't have worried about the latter since the edge of the bridge was protected by a 2 inch high barrier which surely would have prevented our RV from toppling over the side.

I glanced left to see a wall of finely painted brown steel gliding slowly past. I was to discover later that these mobile works of art took 30 gallons of paint in 15 layers, although I am sure that fact would not have offered me much comfort had I known it at the time.

It seemed to go on forever until finally, three miles later the rear of the monstrosity drew level with me. Attached to the rear was an SUV. On top of the SUV was a golf cart. On the back of the SUV was a large box suspended from its tow ball. On the back of the box was attached a motorcycle. Attached to the motorcycle were four push bikes. Attached to the push bikes was a motorized skate board. Attached to the motorized skate board was a pair of inline skates. Then I noticed the 4 kayaks with 80 horsepower outboard motors on the roof of the RV itself.

We encountered this mobile city later at a camp ground. It got there just before us.

Before my eyes, the beast of a machine began transforming.

It grew menacingly in width until it doubled its previous size. Great steel legs descended to the Earth pushing this way and that like a scene from War of the Worlds until the behemoth sat level. A massive satellite receiving dish hummed out of the roof and swiveled into place, locking onto the latest episode of Desperate Housewives.

I was curious to see the type of god-like person who captained such a vast empire of machinery. He would surely be as impressive as his rig.

Emerging shortly after from the complex like a scene from ET came a small fat man with very little hair and more money than God.

It's got the 60' LCD TV times two, full home theatre, wine cellar, central vacuum system, office, Italian tiled floor, laundry, kitchen, bathroom, study, satellite communications systems, free steak knives and the kitchen sink.

'Why so much stuff,?'I enquired.

'I want to feel at home when we rough it,' he replied.

'Wouldn't it be cheaper just to stay home?' I ventured.

He ignored me from then on and proceeded to construct a deck outside complete with awnings and a swimming pool.

The recreation vehicle or RV for short is an ideal way to see the bits of America between the airports. Never having to unpack your bags or risk the charms of cheap roadside motels is a big plus for us. There are campgrounds every few miles which will take the stuff you don't want and give you the stuff you do for a small fee. That means not ever having to use someone else's bathroom or bed.

The roads are long straight and wide and we are not the largest vehicle on the road. These are the 18 wheelers that rumble from one end of the country to the other and across it as well. Each is outfitted with a two bedroom apartment with two bathrooms and a Jacuzzi just behind the driver's seat. They rumble across America until dark then line up at the rest stops on the freeways with their secondary engines running to supply the gigawatts needed to power their small city while they sleep.

Then at the ungodly hour of 5:30am, they start their big engines and let them warm up for 30 minutes while they have the Truckers Breakfast in the nearby cafe that has resulted in truck manufacturers making the gap between the seat and the steering wheel larger. The owner of the tiny 25 foot RV, who had foolishly decided to spend the night there too sandwiched between two of these massive road trains, was suddenly and coincidentally awake at precisely the same moment as the engines bellowed into life. Luckily he had accumulated at least five minutes of sleep throughout the night so the normal grumpiness was hardly in evidence throughout the extended 72 hour day that followed.

5. WEDDING, THE FIRST

Hillary Rodham Clinton is a friend of mine.

When she announced her intention to stand for President, I put my name down as an observer for her first internet rally.

From that moment on, inexplicably, we were close friends. She would let me know by email every day where she was and what she was doing and thank me endlessly for my support. I began to wonder if Bill knew of our relationship and what he might do if he found out. I needn't have worried. Bill is such a friendly guy that he invited me to have lunch with him and Hillary and 5,000 of his closest friends. He did say they were bit strapped with the campaign and such and would it be ok if we could flick him a quick $100,000 to help cover costs. Unfortunately we were busy that day and had to decline. Chelsea too, wrote to me a couple of times to thank me for supporting her mom so loyally. I thought it was sweet.

With such a close relationship developing with the whole family, it came as somewhat of a surprise then that we didn't receive our invitation to Chelsea's wedding on July 31, 2010. It's possible my invitation ended up in my junk mail box and they were simply too busy with the wedding and being Secretary of State and stuff and it simply slipped their minds to follow up with a phone call.

It wouldn't have made any difference anyway since we had a better offer and I would have had to decline once again. (I wonder if these constant refusals are damaging our relationship? It seems odd that I haven't heard from them since Barack Obama whipped her in the primaries.)

Our very dear friends from Chicago whom we met in Portugal 30 years before have two sons, one of whom was getting married himself on that very same day in Wisconsin. So there was no question that we wouldn't be there. This and the wedding of their eldest son three weeks later in San Diego was the reason we travelled to America in the first place and bought an RV.

I pushed Hillary, Chelsea and Bill from my mind as we prepared for the big day. I was at once curious and excited to see how folk in America celebrate a wedding.

On this occasion, organization and planning were the keys to an event that took place over two days beginning with a full rehearsal on the Friday and a rehearsal dinner to be held at a rural golf course. The area being rather remote meant that there were few campgrounds where we could hole up for a couple of days in our RV. The one we chose seemed to be the closest to the action which was taking place at three different venues in rural Wisconsin. When the time came for us to travel in our semi-formal best from the campground to the Golf Club, I programmed the GPS and started the engine. Imagine my surprise when TomTom announced that if I turned left in 250 feet I had reached my destination. Double checking the maps, we discovered the campground bordered the Golf Club.

So we walked there.

The evening featured a well presented slide show of photos of the bride and groom throughout their lives to date. Young people these days know how to pose for photos in such a way that it looks like they were having a whale of a time. Not for them the stiff fixed smiles like the old days. The photos are stage managed to make the viewer believe that the participants were captured in a frenzy of such fun that they, the viewer, could not help but feel somehow inadequate that their lives were not as exciting.

'Didn't they have such fun growing up' commented a teary old aunt sitting near me. 'It wasn't like that in my day.'

'Nostalgia's not what it used to be' I consoled her. 'We really knew how to reminisce back then didn't we?'

I left her to work that one out and went looking for more free wine.

The slide show was followed by dinner then a roast and toast by anyone who had something to say about either of the party.

This filled me with some trepidation since visions of inarticulate, mumbling, drunken young male friends of the groom bringing up lurid episodes of his past life that would mortify everyone there sprang to mind. The shrieking and infantile giggling of drunken, swaying and drink-spilling female friends of the bride falling off their high heels was another fear. Perhaps I just go to the wrong weddings in New Zealand where such hideous behavior occurs, because here my fears were groundless. What followed were thoughtful discourses from intelligent, articulate and well mannered young people that left me with the impression that the world would be in safe hands when it was their turn to run things.

Later that evening a game of 10 pin bowls was organized and it was here that I was able to demonstrate good old kiwi prowess in the sports arena. That my wife and I came last and second to last respectively out of around 30 players in no way diminishes the spectacular nature of my finest shot which brought the crowd to its feet in astonished awe and gasped amazement. The photo below says it all as I put my body on the line for the perfect shot. It would have brought a little tear to the eye of All Black Rugby coach Graeme Henry had he been there.

Slippery shoes, polished floor and very little native ability at the game could have been a contributing factor.

The wedding ceremony itself the next day was performed on the shores of Lake Sinisippi and was simply perfect. Even the weather cooperated with cool, fine conditions. The wedding party consisted of 8 bridesmaids, 8 groomsmen, 5 flower girls and 6 ushers for a total of 27 not counting the mums and dads from both sides. Eat your heart out Chelsea, you only had 26.

There was a reasonably stable pier jutting into the lake from the property and I thought a photo from the end looking back would be an important memory. People who know me will be suddenly alert now as they recall a similar incident at a wedding some 37 years ago in Russell, New Zealand where I fell in the water whilst attempting an important photo opportunity. That they still talk about it up there prompted my wife to warn me not to attempt the feat.

Experience is what you get just after you need it most.

On this occasion, my experience stood me in good stead and the photo was completed without incident.

The reception was a lavish affair and went without a hitch thanks to the superb organizational skills of the ones responsible. The after party dance went well into the night and fell just short of members of the wedding party getting their gear completely off. Many new photos were added to the life story of our happy couple and no doubt will get an airing in times to come as they move through the stages of their lives together.

There are many details of which I am sure I am not aware and for that reason cannot be mentioned here. For example the women guests were asked to dress in black to complement the bridal party who were in black. *Editor's note: By definition this is not an example since you are obviously aware of it otherwise you couldn't have written about it.* Author responds: Picky, very picky.

Three candles were set out in a row; all were properly

shielded from the gentle breeze blowing and were to represent the Bride, the Groom and their new union respectively. The first two caught light as they were meant to, but the candle representing their union sputtered and went out – three times, causing a quiet murmur of consternation to ripple through the assembled witnesses.

Other than that incident, I marked the occasion a resounding success and was thankful I wasn't the one paying the bills.

6. BIKERS ON THE MOVE

We were lucky, or unlucky enough depending on your point of view, to be in the Badlands area of South Dakota just before the annual Sturgis bikers rally whereupon every Harley Davidson ever made descends upon the place to cruise around aimlessly and take up valuable space until it is time to go home and wait for next year.

It was a big one this time, the 70th anniversary. So bikers from all over America descended upon Sturgis and Deadwood, South Dakota for the rally. 800,000 bikers were expected and this is not an exaggeration for literary effect. *Editors Note: I warned you about this. If you continue to stretch the truth no one will believe you when you have something really big to report.* Author's response: I've never let the facts get in the way of a good yarn.

They appeared everywhere like noisy blowflies buzzing in and out of parking lots, gas stations and roadside restaurants.

The typical biker was 65 years old, approaching the legal definition of land whale, with a long grey beard, grey hair tied back in a pony tail, tattoos everywhere that once were fierce eagles but now looked like faded wrinkled sparrows, bandana tied over the head with no helmet, dark glasses and some of the lucky ones - and I use the term generously - had the female version riding pillion. These bad bitches could break ya balls soon as look at ya, or so I was told when caught staring.

The bikers could be categorized into the following 5 Species.

> 1. The previously described biker who never grew up since Easy Rider in 1969 but managed to grow out to impressive proportions. These bad boys rode all the way from where ever it is they came from in

America to cruise, swagger, smoke and generally just trying to look bad like they did in 1969. A small trickle of fear ran up my spine when I first saw an example of this Species. Memories from 1969 when these guys were tough played in my head. Then I noticed the ponderous gut, the arthritic hip and the missing teeth. I can take you now you bastard, I thought to myself, just try to start something. Maybe I'll start something myself like back over your beautiful, clean, shiny Harley while you're at the toilet in the gas station. They make more stops for toilet than gas now. That'll teach them to humiliate poor little skinny white guys in front of their girl friends in 1969 when all I was doing was ... (that wasn't out loud was it?) Then I realized there were another 800,000 of them around and I might have my hands full. The other difference between 1969 and 2010 is the quality of the bikes. Back then they were filthy, oily, dust covered iron horses that rode the trail looking fer trouble. Today they are pristine, gleaming, high quality machines looking fer a place to park outta the sun where the leather work won't fade and not too far from a toilet.

2. Young punks born too late to be bad boys from 1969, but wanna be a part of the action anyway and

pretend. Too bad they had to go back to work after the weekend unlike the real bad boys who could collect their pensions anywhere. These guys failed the grey beard test and didn't need the bandana over the head since their hair was too short. Fail.

3. Bad boys from 1969 who crossed over to the good side, got a job, a mortgage, 2.4 kids and rose to be a partner in their firm. While their Harleys were as pristine and shiny as the others, there was no way they were going to actually ride the thing all the way from the holiday home in Florida or the family estate in Vermont. Hell no! That's what the 48 foot RV was for with the trailer to carry the bikes or the toy hauler RV which has a garage at the back. (you think I'm exaggerating again? Not this time.) *Editor's Note: sigh.* The other method was the custom built trailer behind the fancy pick-up truck traveling in convoy with the family in the RV. Bad Dad could ride in comfort until the last few miles.

We spotted this Species in campgrounds bordering the Bad Lands area of South Dakota. They could safely park their RV at the campground where it would remain out of sight from the real bad boys, pimp themselves out in the old gear that was let out in the middle to accommodate the result of 40 years living the American Dream and ride triumphantly into Deadwood, South Dakota like they had been on the road for a week, then swagger down the street and take over the saloons just like the old days. Unfortunately the lack of grey beard was a dead giveaway. Sorry guys, you're just not scary anymore. Fail.

4. Bitches on Bikes. These are the female version of the above who have taken to riding on the front seat of their own Harley instead of hitching a ride on the back like they did back in '69, although it is probably safer to do so now since it takes everything the old boys have got just to get their leg over their Harley. Their tattoos too are competing with the wrinkles for a place on their skin and the facial hair, while impressive, is not up to the standards set by the old boys. Nevertheless they take their place as equals in the roar up the street and the swagger down the footpath to the saloon. Sorry girls, you just aren't scary either. Well you are but not in the way you wanted.

5. Bikers who ride something other than a Harley. This Species accounted for maybe 5% of the total number of bikes in town. They were not allowed to park them near the Harleys since they were not nearly loud enough nor cool enough. These bikes were smooth, quiet, and looked like RVs on two wheels. Despicable! They should be banned from the event. These outsiders were subsumed into Species 2 and 3 once they dismounted, swaggered into the saloon where their abomination could no longer be associated with them. Not that they could stay hidden for long since all conversations revolved

around the additions and customizations that each Harley owner had made to individualize his machine so he could be unique like everyone else and they had nothing to say.

In the saloons Species 2 and 3 enviously eyed up Species 1 who looked the real deal and who studiously ignored them, recognizing them as the faux bad boys they really are. You sold out, is the unspoken message, don't come near us and no, we won't tell you where the toilets are. Species 4 meanwhile did a sterling job of imitating Species 1. Unfortunately they were ignored by everyone, getting less attention than they did back in '69. But chugging back Buds (Budweisers) gave them something to do that looked a bit like being a bad bitch biker.

Along with the saloons, the pharmacies did a roaring trade. They sold antacids and prescription repeats for heart conditions, arthritis and gout along with a host of other ills. Condoms which were big in '69 seemed to stay on the shelves this time around.

The numbers were staggering. For a week BEFORE the event, bikers were in evidence everywhere in a 200 mile radius of Sturgis and Deadwood, just cruising this way or that. The economy boomed. Everywhere there were signs saying Welcome Bikers, unlike in '69 when they were run out of town by people with short hair cuts and no necks and who are now dead.

The bikers who would destroy a town back then were now content to gather at the local gas station, especially when it rained and they could park their bikes under the roof in numbers so great other motorists could not get to the pumps. This also gave them the opportunity to use the toilet and pimp out their bikes a little while they waited for the rain to stop. Out came the polish rags and wheel rims were lovingly restored to the gleaming perfection they had been before. Then they would exit without destroying the place in a roar that would register on the Richter Scale 1,000 miles away and leave it at that. The shopkeepers and innkeepers weren't fooled. The sound of 800,000 Harleys was unable to drown out the sound of ringing tills.

Harley Davidson is an American icon. No other company has such loyalty that their customers will tattoo their logo onto their skin, although I was tempted to get a Diet Coke one while I was there.

The name in the popular vernacular has been shortened to simply Harley. Now if I were Davidson, I would be mightily pissed off. When they decided on the name for the new company, little did Davidson know how important being first would become. 'Yeah, my Davidson has the extended pipe,' seems more like a conversation you would hear at an agricultural show.

By the time we got to Deadwood, we had learned the rules of the road in America, especially what happens when you meet other vehicles. While the card you fill out at 36,000 feet on the way in providing the information the Customs and Immigration Officials demand, contains lots of valuable information such as from which country you boarded your vessel and if you belong to a terrorist group, (that one has surely thwarted many attempts to commit terrorism in the United States – 'Damn, they're on to me, didn't see that one coming at our training camps in Afghanistan. Nothing I can do now other than surrender.'), they provide no clues as to how to drive a vehicle in America or who gives way to whom. You learn that on the fly.

The rule of the uncontrolled intersection is both simple and effective: Give way to anyone who might have a gun or a good lawyer. Bluff has always been an effective tool in my life and this rule is made for me. Waving the 'L' sign out the window as you approach the intersection will invariably bring all traffic to a stop allowing you instant clear access. The NRA or National Rifle Association logos plastered all over the vehicle don't seem to impede my progress either.

If we ever go to Texas where they don't bother with 'L' signs but simply wave their weapon out of the window, I will probably remove them.

Editors note: Do not try these techniques in Texas as they will more than likely end in a gun fight.

My experience with Texans goes back 20 years when I was doing business with a small, family owned Houston company. After being ushered into the President's office by a land whale, the first thing I noted was the collection of game trophies stuck to the walls between a giant American flag and an even larger Texan flag.

'I like what you've done with the heads,' I remarked to the youngish President of the company who wore a ten gallon hat that would have made John Wayne a proud man, but which on him made his own head look quite small.

'Wah, thank yew,' he replied. 'Ah jus looove to go huntin', fishin' an shootin' ever chance ah can git.'

'Where did you get the bear head?' I asked. 'I thought there were no bears left in Texas.'

'Mah granddaddy shot that fellah in Utah when he was a young un'. It was the last bear in the state,' he announced proudly.

'Maybe you too will shoot the last of something one day,' I offered, appalled.

'That would be great,' he agreed, 'but you would never know it for a long time now would you?'

That was as philosophical as the conversation was destined to go.

Air travel is the quickest way out of Texas.

7. YELLOWSTONE

Yellowstone National Park is the Rotorua of the United States but with animals and without Maori; or Indian for that matter, currently known as Native Americans, who once lived there and apparently are not welcome as part of the natural environment unlike the bison, deer, elk, bears, chipmunks, squirrels etc.

Yellowstone National Park is about 100 miles wide and long and devoted to showcasing what is left of North American wildlife and the natural thermal wonders scattered around the park.

A largely successful conservation job has been achieved at the same time as allowing the hundreds of thousands of human visitors annually to see the animals in an almost natural environment and the physical attractions of the area as well.

So successful has been the program that the animals ignore the thousands of humans entering their environment and treat them as neither a threat nor an opportunity, thus allowing people to see them close up and apparently unaffected by civilization.

By close up I mean wandering across the road in front of your vehicle without bothering to look both ways or wait for a gap in the traffic. Such occurrences are easy to spot as traffic comes to a halt and queues of a thousand miles in both directions form instantly. So you know that somewhere in the far distance up ahead of you, an animal is crossing the road or munching in an adjacent field and the lucky ones at the head of the queue are clambering out of their vehicles to take photos and begin mentally composing stories for their envious friends, work mates, neighbors, strangers on the street and relatives that they can retell until the cows come home.

Oblivious to the chaos they are causing in downtown Denver, they stay in the middle of the road long after the animal has disappeared, excitedly giving each other the first version of their Great Story which will surely grow in the telling for years to come.

Of course by the time the traffic moves again, the animal would be nowhere to be seen, but fortune favors the lucky and near dusk we came upon a queue of just a dozen or so vehicles. The animal, which turned out to be a small grizzly bear, was wandering through the trees beside the road towards us thus depriving the early arrivers of their pole position. We were by a clearing in the trees when the bear emerged just yards away from us allowing me a first class photo opportunity which I took, praying that the camera wouldn't develop a flat battery or similar. By the time the bear had wandered off into the forest I was mentally composing the story I would tell my friends, work mates, neighbors, strangers on the street and relatives when I got home, oblivious to the fact that the vehicles in front of me had long since moved off and I was the one at the head of the queue causing the chaos in Seattle.

The standard way of meeting and greeting the animals is to keep your eyes peeled as you enter the park. You begin to see all sorts of bears, elk, coyotes and bison far away on the horizon which turn into tree stumps when you zoom in to take a look. Then after a while you spot a small herd of bison about 2 miles away across a large meadow. You quickly get out of your vehicle and stumble carefully across the meadow to get closer so you can get a photo that isn't just a blur on the horizon, avoiding the rattlesnakes which must surely be in every small bush your unprotected foot brushes against.

After walking several miles, you finally get to a spot where you get a reasonable photo using a little telephoto so as not to scare the animal by getting too close and allowing what you hope should be enough room to run in case they attack. Then you trudge back to your vehicle, avoiding the rattlesnakes that missed you on the way in, and triumphantly begin composing your Great Story.

You set off again and around the next corner the road is blocked by a massive herd of bison wandering in front of your vehicle which are neither scared of you nor inclined to attack.

Behavior of the humans is controlled by the Park Rangers who outnumber the bison 10 to 1. Signs everywhere say don't feed the animals, don't approach them, get out of their way, stay on the tracks, don't park there, don't litter, don't leave food out, watch your mouth, and I'll let you off with a warning this time but if you park on the gravel footpath again or break another rule, you will get a ticket. Your details have been logged and every Park Ranger in the country is now aware of you and your criminal tendencies, so watch yourself. Have a nice day.

A placid herd of elk were sheltering from the sun in the shadows on a hotel lawn. The footpath nearby had been closed with signs and orange cones to keep the people away from them. Having already photographed two small elk on a distant hill using maximum telephoto capability, we saw no need to engage this lot so we affected a bored, world-weary kind of demeanor, ignoring the animals. I was sure this would impress the lesser tourists gawking away with their cameras clicking as we nonchalantly wandered past the herd to the nearby bar. The beer was cool and satisfying.

Emerging some time later it seemed the elk were on the move. The footpath was still closed but other areas were rapidly becoming no-go places as the elk moved. Naturally they decided to move towards the footpath we were using.

'Get outta there, get away, NOW!' screamed the nearby park ranger. Not knowing where to go since the footpaths and roads were either closed or being occupied by elk which didn't seem to have an opinion about us one way or another, we stood rooted to the spot while the Park Ranger advanced menacingly on us.

'GET OUT!' he screamed again.

'We were here first,' I protested.

'They were here thousands of years before you got here,' he snapped, 'and it's their park.'

They didn't look that old to me and it was a guy in a uniform similar to my tormentor's that took money off me when I entered the park rather than an elk, but we moved anyway trying to get back to our RV.

'GET AWAY FROM THERE!' screamed another Park Ranger. Since we were now in the middle of the road and surrounded by elk and Park Rangers, it seemed we had nowhere to go. The elk were concerned neither about us nor the screaming going on around them.

'We're not interested in the elk,' we protested,

'We just want to get back to our RV and away from the screaming.'

'We own a thousand of these on our farm in New Zealand,' my wife lied. Before the Rangers could reach for their guns, the elk solved the issue by meandering somewhere else leaving us to walk meekly back to our RV.

The Park Ranger, whose job it was to follow the elk with a shovel and a bucket to pick up their poop from the pristine lawn, then accosted some more unfortunate tourists who stumbled unwittingly too close to his charges. Armed with a sidearm, a radio on his belt, a shovel and a bucket full of poop, he did not seem to be having a good day. I wondered if he had been turned down for a job with the metro police and following tame elk and awaiting their bowel movements was as good as he could get. At least he had a gun.

Relaxing in our RV, another commotion broke out soon after. The elk, which according to the signs, were dangerous wild animals and free to roam where they wished, were being mustered. Our Park Ranger was whistling and calling to them and directing them into a corral for the night. Most of them complied by being bribed with a little reward hidden in the Ranger's hand.

Those among you who are farmers will know that there are always a couple of animals in the herd that won't cooperate. This herd was no exception and we were treated to the delightful sight of the Park Ranger, who had taken exception to my choice of parking and who had said we were fortunate to have an RV thus taking our home with us, so it's too bad there aren't enough parks for you, get used to it; trying to run down two elk that disagreed with both the timing and destination chosen by the Rangers. *Editors note: This type of mustering is best done with dogs that are not encumbered with bulky uniforms, guns, radios and buckets of poop and that can run faster than Park Rangers.*

Nevertheless a bucket of poop thrown at elk can have a sobering effect on them and the Park Rangers prevailed.

I wondered if I had once again landed unknowingly in a theme park, this time one full of circus animals. Curiously the exact same number of suspiciously similar wild animals was happily lounging on another lawn just a block away the next day, with the same Poop Ranger in attendance.

I did have a close encounter of the chipmunk kind earlier that day at our campsite though that was not staged as far as I could tell.

In his/her search for food, my gnarled and tanned foot must have looked like the base of a tree. The quick moving little creature scampered over to me while I stood rigidly still, reached out a tiny paw and touched me lightly on the big toe. Quickly deciding there was no future in that particular exploration it scampered off to investigate the wheel arch of a nearby car. It all happened so quickly that no photo was possible even though the camera was in my hand and fully armed. I do however have some vaguely interesting shots of empty ground and part of the wheel of someone's car if anyone would like copies.

We left the mayhem at the hotel behind us to find the hot spring river we had been told about earlier that could be used for bathing. Having found it, there was nowhere to park an RV legally and I was concerned about the wrath of the Yellowstone Park Rangers descending upon me if I parked illegally again. We decided to backtrack to a place further up the hill where a small hot stream flowed near a legal RV park.

Stripping down to our swimming trunks we were soon semi submerged in a shallow but fast running, perfectly hot stream that soothed away the day's cares. Not knowing whether or not this activity would be sanctioned by the bossy Park Rangers, we kept a wary eye out. We didn't have to wait long for her to cruise by in her squad car.

'Stay down,' I hissed to my wife and we flattened ourselves into the bed of the stream like escaped convicts.

Foolishly the Ranger failed to glance to her right and she cruised away blissfully ignorant of the opportunity that had just slipped unknowingly from her grasp.

'She didn't see us,' I gloated. 'Why don't we use some rocks and make a small dam to create a nice pool?'

'Don't push your luck,' my wife warned.

While much of the park is underwhelming to New Zealand born eyes used to scenes of stunning natural beauty and thermal activity, we were truly gob smacked by the scene that unfolded before us at Mammoth Hot Springs.

Before our astonished eyes, we beheld the awesome wonder that must compare with the lost Pink and White Terraces of

Tarawera, New Zealand, once considered the eighth natural wonder of the world, but destroyed in a volcanic eruption in 1886.

Acres of delicate silica and minerals had formed themselves into beautiful terraces of blinding, pure white and deep oranges, holding pools of azure blue waters that cascaded down the mountainside.

Unlike the Pink and White Terraces, which in their day attracted visitors from around the world who bathed carelessly in them, these were sensibly 'look but don't touch' attractions. Boardwalks that allowed the visitor to explore all parts of this incredible field of terraces without making contact with it had been constructed in such a way that they did not detract from the natural beauty before us.

It was another fine example that Yellowstone seems to do so well of allowing people to get close without their presence affecting the thing being studied.

We bedded down that night in the park to the sound of yapping coyotes in the nearby hills.

The next day was geyser day for us. With the anticipation of Old Faithful awaiting us the following day, we eagerly tramped over hill and dale in search of magnificent geysers.

We were to be disappointed. The geysers seemed frail and weak with very little spurt, sort of like geezers instead. The signs boasted of past prowess that they might be able to display again sometime in the future if only people hadn't ruined it for them in the past...

Wait a minute. That was the old geezer at the pub the night

before.

The excitement of the day was once again provided by the animals and the traffic jams. A grizzly bear wandered alongside the road ripping fallen tree trunks apart in search of grubs but had to make do with flowers. A study of trees torn apart in this manner later revealed not soft rotten trunks as one would expect, but hard wood that would need a chisel to cut into it. That the bear could rip this tree apart with one raking swipe of its front paw and three inch claws was a reminder of how powerful and dangerous these creatures are and the thought of an encounter with them was enough to send a shiver up my spine.

12 pointed stag elk were seen grazing across the river much to the delight of around 150 clicking spectators and to the chagrin of 10,000 would-be spectators stuck in the traffic jam that stretched to the horizon.

Arriving back at camp we were given the disturbing but thrilling news that a mother grizzly with two cubs was making her way through the camp and we were to stay near our vans for safety. It might have been a bedtime story to keep us in our vans and it worked.

Old Faithful is so-called because it erupts on a regular basis every 60 to 90 minutes unlike the other geysers in the park that are a bit fussy and irregular. It was our last stop in Yellowstone and we arrived to find out that, according to the hand written sign outside the kiosk, the next eruption was due at 1:41pm, 90 minutes away.

So we wandered the rest of the area taking in the sights and the crowd grew steadily until there were 3.2 million people encircling Old Faithful waiting expectantly for the show to start.

Suspiciously right on schedule at 1:41pm, and I'm sure I heard the rumbling of machinery from deep underground, Old Faithful let rip with an enormous fountain of steam and water that must have reached 300 feet in height. It lasted around three minutes and when it was over, everyone rushed for their car or the gigantic RV that was blocking us from making a quick getaway ourselves. It was like coming out of a football game with the traffic jam to match as we spent the next five and a half hours inching towards the exit of the car park.

Unlike the geezers, this geyser was impressive and gave us the best three minutes of our trip. We almost wanted to take up smoking to celebrate.

8. OFFICIALS OF THE UNITED STATES

When you visit the United States you will encounter officials in every activity you care to name.

From the moment you disembark from your plane in the United States of America you will be stopped by an official who will want your information and your compliance with whatever it is they are charged with enforcing. It will continue through every museum, toll bridge, animal shelter, ski lift, road works site and supermarket in the land. It will not end until the captain of your plane tells you to remain in your seat until the aircraft has come to a complete stop at the terminal in Auckland.

This is the land of the free - provided you do as you're told.

Every facet of American life seems to be enforced by rules and regulations that define your very existence and there is an army of officials eager and ready to challenge your right to exist and force you to prove it whenever needed.

She'll be right mate, ya look pretty damned honest to me, does not cut the mustard here.

Officials can be defined as those people who can legally impose themselves on you and interact with you without your consent or ability to do anything about it.

They come in three categories:

1. Those that love their jobs and try to squeeze every ounce of pleasure they can from it. This includes making you do things you probably don't have to do and stopping you from doing things that you probably can such as standing on the wrong side of the queue line. This category includes frustrated individuals who tried and failed to get a proper job

like policeman/woman, marine sergeant, bank manager, secret agent, CIA assassin, conqueror of anti-American upstart countries or benevolent, right-thinking dictator of their own country. This category likes military-style uniforms best and the War on Terror has given those in the right industry a massive boost in self esteem and the ability to exercise more power for power's sake. They can be identified by an over-zealous approach to their job and may add unnecessary bits to it to make the pleasure last just a little longer.

They don't care about you or your problems.

2. Those that hate their jobs and take it out on their victims by the unbridled exercise of whatever little power they have. This type likes to humiliate their unfortunate customers, especially in front of others. They are easily identified by their bored expressions, sarcasm, eye rolling, the slow pace at which they do their job and they way they ignore you when you try to stop them for information. No one wants to be married to this type. A good place to find these officials is in minor public buildings or airports where bags have to be checked with sticks and plastic gloves for the entire 8 hours of their shift.

They too don't care about you or your problems.

3. Those that do their job with a minimum of fuss and are pleasant, polite and helpful when required.

There are none of these in America.

CASE STUDY #1

'Urrr!' grunted the huge, deformed man standing against a wall in the entrance to the local Wal-Mart store as I entered.

'Don't look at him,' I told myself, 'he's huge, deranged and possibly as dangerous as a grizzly bear.'

'Urrrr!' he roared again and began lumbering towards me.

'It's worse than I thought,' I thought, 'he's a Mormon, or even worse than that. It's Amway!' Alarmed, I adopted the defensive 'watchyerself-buddy' posture as he approached.

'Sir,' he called to me for the third time, 'you can't take your own bag into the store.'

I looked at the plastic bag that contained the faulty goods I had just purchased from that same store and understood immediately. He was a Wal-Mart official disguised as a huge, deformed, deranged man selling Amway standing against a wall and with sweeping eyes that saw everything.

Annoyed that a Wal-Mart Neanderthal had scared the living daylights out of me, I swung onto the offensive.

'I'm bringing back the broken, good-for-nothing product that this store just sold me, so watchyerself fellah, I know some good people,' I countered.

'In that case,' he blandly responded quite unlike any Neanderthal I had previously encountered, 'I will need to tag your bag.'

My plastic bag, containing a cell phone I couldn't activate, was duly tagged and was now certified for re-entry into Wal-Mart. Uncomfortably, I felt somewhat elevated by this status that had been endowed upon me. I thought maybe I should wander the aisle for a while and then attempt to leave via a non-checkout lane. That would surely attract the attention of the Official In Charge Of Stopping People Leaving The Store With Plastic Bags That Have Not Been Through A Checkout. Then I could triumphantly wave the accreditation attached to my plastic bag in their face and wallow in their impotence as I swaggered nonchalantly out of the place, my revenge complete and my pride restored.

Then I realized that the cheap phone that I had bought twenty minutes before would still not be working, my victory would be in vain and I would still have to negotiate passage past the Neanderthal to get a phone that worked.

So I meekly reported myself to the Customer Service Desk which is peopled by even more officials, to plead my case for a phone that worked. After filling out the proper forms in triplicate and submitting to their eminence, I was awarded a phone that did what they originally said it would do and this, for some reason, filled me with servile gratitude. To rub salt into the wounds, no one had called me on it over a week later, but I got a small amount of satisfaction through ringing my voice mail and changing it from time to time.

CASE STUDY #2

The tires crackled on the gravel road as the five year old Chevrolet compact cruised slowly and ominously through the nearly deserted, tree lined State Park campground beside a delightful stream in north east Utah, a lightly populated area that surely needed officials to keep control. Of the seven bare camping sites with no facilities, there were two with occupants. One set in a modest and decent tent on site 3, the other in a giant, obscene 25 foot RV with Florida plates and no sticker attached to the tree on site 6.

Lois and Harold, the local Utah State Park Officials plus their Shitsu, (particularly ugly and tiny, vicious dog with, as Lois was later to admit, a bad haircut) were on the hunt for campers who had done everything right by filling in the form at the self registration post, putting $13 in the envelope, tearing off the correct portion of the supplied ticket and clipping it to the tree on their chosen camp site that was the freedom to which they were entitled.

Luckily for Lois, the most intrepid of the trio, the bastards at site 6 of 7 had failed to comply and were displaying absolutely nothing on their tree!

Sensing a plot that might herald the end of the Republic and wondering if she should call for back up, Lois slid down her window to fearlessly face this latest menace.

'Are you Site 6,' she demanded with lips pursed like a cat leaving the room?

'I am,' I admitted.

'You didn't fill out the form, place $13 in the envelope, tear off your portion of the registration card and clip it to the tree at your chosen site which is the freedom to which you are entitled,' she accused, looking at me like I must have been from another state, while Harold grinned helplessly and the Shitsu whose name turned out to be Cyril, snarled at me menacingly, threatening to take off a fingernail.

'Correct,' I responded, looking back at her as if I was from another country. 'I knew you would be around sooner or later so I thought I would wait and give it to you in person, besides, I never saw anything that looked like an envelope or instructions on how to park in a campground that's unserviced apart from a hole in the ground purporting to be a fireplace but with no fire wood.'

Lois' mouth pursed even further as if she were chewing on a wasp with a side order of sour lemon and I knew I was in deep trouble.

'You must have your official ticket attached to the designated tree beside the camping place of your choice within 30 minutes of your arrival at the State Park,' she intoned officially, 'You should have proceeded down the gravel road at the top where the envelopes and signs with the official rules of the camp are fully displayed in sharp contrast to the peaceful and serene surroundings of the forest, burbling stream and carefree birds,' she admonished.

'Great Balls Of Fire,' I exclaimed! (Actually I think I said the 'f' word but that is not acceptable in Utah I discovered after Cyril attempted to remove the second knuckle of the middle finger of my gesticulating right hand) 'I must have missed the official top gravel road and come in at the unofficial bottom gravel road that didn't contain such explicit instructions,' I took delight in explaining with barely disguised derision for the administrative cock-up that could result in a person being able to enter the park with impunity through an unofficial and unsanctioned avenue in what Homeland Security would obviously view as a further opportunity to place another few thousand officials with bag-delving sticks and metal-detecting rods at entrances to similar unprotected parks throughout the country, if only they knew about them.

I began to spank myself in admonition while Harold giggled like a little girl.

'What kind of dog is that?' I enquired while it glared at me with bulging eyes, hoping I would get within striking range of a fatal nip.

'It's a Shitsu' responded Lois.

'Is that Japanese for a crap dog,' I enquired?

'I don't know,' she replied, 'I got it from my son two months ago. It's about 8 years old.'

'Why doesn't your son like you,' I wondered aloud?

'Y'all need to be payin' ye're $13,' said Lois getting back to business and instructed Harold to leave the safety of the compact Chevrolet to boldly collect the money.

'Are you a volunteer,' I queried the obviously long suffering and quite old Harold?

'Hell no, Ah get paid to do this joab,' he boasted, 'uthawahse ah wouldn't do it.'

'Good fer you, you go get em,' I encouraged. In his official State Park uniform, he looked like an aging boy scout in long pants.

Lois and Cyril meanwhile remained secure in the compact Chevrolet even though the window was down inviting a vicious attack which even Cyril would have been hard pressed to repel. Fearlessly they held their ground and fixed me with a baleful stare.

'You know we're from New Zealand and we are good people,' I whined pathetically to Lois.

'Oh yeah,' she rejoined intelligently.

'You know where New Zealand is,' I enquired?

'Sure, I've heard of it, I've seen it.' Something in the way she shifted uncomfortably in her seat alerted me to the possibility that she didn't know much about the world beyond Utah. I moved in for the kill.

'Tell me where it is,' I challenged.

'Oh. Ah don't know nuttin' 'bout history,' she countered lamely.

'How about geography,' I replied? 'Any luck there?'

'Ah don't know nuttin' 'bout geography neither, but ah do know y'all should have put the thirt-teen dollahs in the box, filled out the form, and stuck your card on the tree... Is that a fah there y'all got?' she demanded, eyeing our camp fire for which we had had to scavenge through 500 acres of forest for sufficient dry wood to get it burning. 'Don't let that fah get too hah otherwise it'll burn down the fore-rest.'

This sudden change in tactics to bring the battle back to her territory took me momentarily by surprise. I grimly realized my opponent was smarter than I had given her credit for and I knew I would have to dig deep to regain a tactical advantage.

'Is Cyril a good dog,' I enquired by way of counter attack?

'He don't much like males,' she sniffed, falling blindly into my trap.

Now being a dog whisperer from way back, I decided to test the loyalty of her Shitsu just to piss her off. The smell of a freshly cooked piece of marinated chicken on the end of my right index finger proved too much for Cyril when I offered him a sniff and he was mine. This seemed to be positive proof to Lois that if I was not the Devil himself, then I was his second-in-command. Harold meanwhile was processing the $13 cash we had had ready for their inevitable arrival and Cyril wanted to come home with me.

Having triumphed in her quest to neutralize the threat to the Republic and secure the $13 for the State, Lois prepared to leave before she got too far behind. To her annoyance, Harold had filled out the forms on my behalf during the battle and had stuck the ticket on the tree for me. No doubt he would be hearing from her on the way home on this breach of official procedure.

'Don't let that fah get too hah,' she warned, getting in the last word as the compact Chevrolet pulled out of the Park using the official gravel track for exiting.

CASE STUDY #3

'Drive! Drive! Drive!' Screamed the official holding what we call the lollypop sign at the road works, except that this one didn't say Stop/Go. It said Stop/Slow. My wife, who was driving, thus letting me off any responsibility regarding the following story, had been cruising slowly through a road works area of Yellowstone National Park and couldn't help admiring the craftsmanship and skill of the workers building a stone wall on the side of the road.

Her pace was obviously not to the liking of the Stop/Slow official and the business of America must be kept moving despite the need for the appreciation of art in action. Rather than put her foot down as was demanded, she stopped completely and asked if the Slow side of the lollipop referred to the IQ of the holder and if this was sufficient reason to forgive the rude outburst of the same. Fortunately the

Stop/Slow official was not in the class of official that can command a gun so my wife's insult was either forgiven or it went over his head. Whichever way it was, the artistes continued their magnificent work and we continued our journey south, with the disruption to the business of America being inconsequential.

CASE STUDY #4

The bored, enormously fat, ugly latino woman behind the counter at the gas station looked at me when I entered like I had just crawled out of an oozing, green, pit of particularly unpleasant slime. What the fuck do you want, she looked, although not a word passed the fat greasy lips which had allowed many a grease burger with triple cheese, extra large fries and a sooper dooper orange mango, biggy sized shake in a jumbo bucket you get to take home free, to pass where words had not.

'The card reader at the pump is faulty,' I said by way of introduction. Rolling her eyes into the back of her pudgy face and making a sigh that sounded like Darth Vader's last wheeze, was her way of saying, of course it is, we put the badly handwritten paper sign over the card reader so idiots like you couldn't stick their card in it and you have to come in here to face me. I don't like you, she looked, and no-one in here likes you either.

I handed over my National Bank Debit TravelCard which the nice lady at the bank in New Zealand had said was accepted anywhere that Mastercard was, but clearly wasn't in many places throughout the United States.

She checked it for unpleasant, crawly things that might attach themselves to her and make her day even worse before sliding it through her card reader which didn't have a handwritten sign across it.

'I'll need some photo ID,' she sneered ungraciously.

'Don't need it,' I countered. 'I can use a pin.' With barely disguised hatred, she pushed a greasy, dirty, disease-ridden keypad in front of me.

'Declined!' She bellowed in obvious delight loud enough to be heard in the next County. Traffic came to a sudden stop and people glared accusingly at me to register their disgust and loathing. The short, stocky and very wide security guard with a triangular head and the marine haircut, pulled the microphone attached to his lapel towards his face, tilted his head as far as it would go given that he had no neck and it was attached directly to his shoulders, and barked some military-type words into his collar while he looked grimly in my direction. I noted there was no return crackle and he didn't have anything in his ear. He fingered his gun in anticipation and I could see a vein pulsing in what passed for his neck at the tantalizing prospect of some action against a middle aged, out of shape white guy.

'Must be the damned bank again,' I muttered in embarrassment as I snatched back the card and returned to the RV for a credit card. 'Give me yours,' I said to my wife since mine had developed a partial split through the magnetic strip and would have given my nemesis further ammunition to humiliate me.

I handed it over.

'I'll need to see some photo ID,' she demanded.

'Great Balls of Fire!' I thought. 'It's my wife's card!'

I could see myself spending the next 20 years in Leavenworth.

'Hold on,' I muttered stalling for time. I grabbed the card back and fled the building with a spot burning on the back of my neck as I anticipated the inevitable impact of the security guard's bullet which I knew was on its way.

Luckily his shot missed and I reached the safety of the RV.

'They need photo ID,' I whined to my wife, 'you'll have to go.'

Bravely, she marched into harm's way and exited a moment later signaling that I should start pumping the gas.

BERNIE COOK

9. A NASTY ENCOUNTER

A close encounter with invisible insects during the after dance party of the wedding in Wisconsin revealed another facet of American culture worth a mention.

That mosquitoes from around the world find me highly desirable is a burden I have carried all my life. People who know me well often seek to sit with me at outdoor parties. This is not for the scintillating or effulgent conversation I may be able to offer, nor the keenness of my razor sharp wit that attracts others to me. No, I keep the mosquitoes away from them.

It began like any other encounter I have had with mosquitoes. I slowly became aware that I was scratching itches on various parts of my exposed skin. One bite on my elbow quickly became the size of a golf ball much to my alarm. Home spun remedies were quickly offered by those around me who were secretly pleased it was not them that had been bitten. 'My grandmother used to rub vinegar on it' offered one helpfully despite knowing that vinegar was not on the menu that day.

'Try rubbing it with salt' suggested another. 'It always worked for my grandfather's second cousin's friend apparently.'

This seemed worth a try and after a few minutes of rubbing salt into the wound, most of the skin on my elbow had disappeared leaving it not only swollen but sore and an ugly red color as well.

'I have just the thing' whispered a woman close to me.

Out of her handbag she produced a plastic bag with a small quantity of suspicious looking white powder in it.

Glancing around nervously to see if anyone was watching, I said, 'Is that what I think it is?'

'This is just a little, it should do the job and I have more back in my room' she whispered conspiritoriously.

'What is it?' I asked, dreading the reply and wondering if there were DEA agents amongst the guests.

'Meat tenderizer' she said. 'It works a treat. Dissolve some of this in wine and rub it in'

'Red or white?' I asked, relieved.

'I'd go with the white' she suggested.

'Any particular reason?' I asked thinking about the possible chemical reactions of tannin on meat tenderizer or some other such sage reason that might have been handed down to her through generations of folk wisdom.

'I'm drinking the red' she replied.

While the thought of putting something on my arm that is used to make a steak tastier was more than a little disturbing to me and caused unbidden images of my arm on a barbeque to come flooding into my mind, the golf ball-sized bite was becoming increasingly painful and larger, so I was prepared to try anything at this stage short of amputation above the elbow.

As it happened, it actually worked and the swelling reduced almost immediately.

I was hooked.

'Can you get me some more of this stuff?' I asked confident in the knowledge that I had discovered the solution to my life long battle with mosquitoes.

'No problem' she said, 'I'll just pop up to my room where I keep my stash.'

A few days later they struck again. This time on my face and once again, I didn't see them coming or going. As soon as the golf ball started growing on my cheek below my right eye, I confidently applied the meat tenderizer in the approved manner.

To my horror, it had no effect this time. The swelling grew until my right eye was nearly closed and part of my inner ear thought it was being ejected from the position it had occupied for over half a century.

A visit to the doctor confirmed an infection which needed immediate antibiotics.

'We'll need to give you a quick jab to get it started' advised the doctor who placed me in the care of Nurse Ruthless Mengele, a close relative of Hitler's murderess doctor Josef Mengele. She thrust a syringe the size of King Arthur's lance into my butt and because the pain was merely excruciating, proceeded to rub it with an enormous, calloused thumb until it was unbearable.

'That should do it' she smirked. She was right. It felt like I had been kicked by a mule.

'That hurt,' I complained. She stifled her yawn in faux sympathy and told me that it would at least take my mind off my face for a while.

Two days later the battle of the bugs was stalemated, No improvement but it was no worse, so I surrendered myself to a doctor in the next town.

'You've been bitten by a no-see-um' he said intelligently and went on to explain that it was a mosquito-like insect with a nasty bite.

'Why is it called a no-see-um?' I asked.

'Because it's so small you can't see it' he replied looking at me as if I was an idiot.

'I've never heard of it' I replied looking back as if I wasn't.

'You'll need antibiotics,' he said. 'We'll need to give you a quick jab to get it started.'

It took several minutes for the nurse to drag me out from under the doctor's desk after which I was obliged to offer my other butt for the agony I knew was to follow.

This time however my angel of mercy was just that. She delivered the shot to my seriously clenched butt with a gentleness that contrasted completely with the earlier experience and I was so relieved I offered to marry her on the spot.

Not all nasty experiences hurt. Some are just plain terrifying. Lightning can be a beautiful thing when seen from a distance and followed a minute later by a deep gentle rumble that echoes through the sky. It makes you think of rainy nights, tucked up in front of warm fires, wrapped in cozy blankets and sipping hot milk drinks before settling down in a lovely soft bed and being lulled to sleep by the gentle sound of distant thunder knowing that the following day will be fresh and clean with birds singing beautifully in the trees.

But when it crashes around you in almost constant strikes and rattles the windows of your RV as you try to keep it on the road in a howling gale that appeared out of nowhere seemingly in an instant and when you happen to be on the highest point on a plateau and a lightning strike is imminent, you believe your time on Earth is at an end.

This was the case on the plains of South Dakota where a bright sunny day can quickly turn into a life-threatening storm that engulfs everything in its path.

What started out as a fascinating drive through the Bad Lands where we saw wonderful water-scoured landscapes formed eons ago and beautiful prairies teeming with three or four animals, turned into a terrifying nightmare when a sudden storm struck out of nowhere.

We saw it coming of course and marveled at the frequency of the lightning strikes in the distance but before we knew it, it was on us and we were right in the middle of it on the highest point of land with bolts striking almost continuously around us.

I was told as a child that any lightning that you see or hear has not killed you. You apparently don't see the one that does. This was both comforting and concerning. Comforting because each one we saw was a miss. Aha! Concerning in that if we did get hit and killed we wouldn't know and that must create problems for us of some kind, but we were not sure what.

The best strategy seemed to be to get the hell out of there as quickly as possible. This was a lot harder than it sounded due to the gale force side wind threatening to blow us off the road, so it was 10 miles per hour swerving to and fro across the road.

Ahead in the driving rain I spotted another RV trying to do the same thing and headed in the same direction. It was definitely bigger than ours I noted, and a little taller. Excellent! I thought to myself. I will get up close and the lightning will hit them instead since they are closer to the sky than us and lightning takes the shortest route to the ground according to the myth I was taught at school.

Getting closer involved a risky dash at high speed - namely 20 miles per hour - in the gale to close the gap.

The life or death dash to safety took an agonizingly long time to complete with the RV being buffeted across the road in alarming and desperate maneuvers that were probably more risk to life and limb than the lightning. By the time we reached the imagined safety of the other RV, the storm had passed over as quickly as it had arrived and I concluded from the fact that I was witnessing this that we had survived unscathed.

We descended from the 9,000 feet elevation of the Badlands to the relative safety of Jackson Hole many thousands of feet lower. Why it is called that is beyond me since it seemed quite a nice place.

Like other similar sized towns, it obviously had no real industry, so it turned itself into a living museum to celebrate its past.

The result is a lovely little town with plenty of bars and restaurants with western themes. My personal favorite was the Million Dollar Cowboy Bar. Not only were there real cowboys in there – at least I think they were but their jeans and stirrups looked a might too clean to belong to real cowboys – but the bar stools were saddles on poles. Now that was fun. I'm sure I wouldn't have fallen off if they had provided reins attached to the bar.

10. SALT LAKE CITY

If there was ever a place in the world that deserved to be smote from the face of the Earth, then Salt Lake City is it. Were I God, it would be my first job come Monday morning. It would be gone by lunch time.

The surrounding area looks either like a mistake or God's dumping ground. I mean who in their right mind would build a city right next to a dried up old lake with nothing but salt for company then declare it their promised land?

The Mormons, that's who.

The cunning plan may have been that nobody would dare to follow them there and they could wallow in their polygamy practices without interference.

Sadly for them, their religious freedom to enslave woman was taken from them by the Federal Government.

The conservative religious streak seems to have held on however in such laws as the State of Utah being the only entity that can sell liquor outside of a bar of which there aren't many of those either.

'Is everyone in Salt Lake City a Moron, sorry, Mormon?' I asked of the man behind the counter of the State Liquor Store. He pulled up like I had just slapped him in the face and replied,

'Hell no, I was born here and I'm not a Mormon.'

'Good for you,' nodded the woman behind us.

While the Tabernacles rose majestically into the sky and gleamed with the accumulated wealth tithed by the believers, the rest of the city, presumably where the tithers themselves lived, seemed to be a broken down counterpoint to them. The car fleet was old and worn out and the few people I saw on the streets walked by slouched over as if they had no hope.

That charismatic men calling themselves prophets, spiritual leaders or whatever can enthrall so many people with mind-bending dogma and end up simply enriching themselves at the cost to their flock in the name of God, continues to amaze me. History abounds with examples of this all over the world. In the Duomo of Milan, Italy I was astonished to see a gold and jewel encrusted tomb containing the remains of an Archbishop. So rich was his final resting place that it was sealed behind bars and glass. A nearby tourist remarked that Jesus, in whose name it was built, only got a cave.

To me, Salt Lake City looked to belong in the same category.

Best strategy was to get the Hell out of there which we did.

North of Salt Lake City is the small town of Montpellier which has a delightful, small museum dedicated mainly to the fact that the Oregon Trail split into two trails in the vicinity with the left turn taking pioneers to California and the right turn taking them to Oregon. A series of paintings by a local painter depicted the hardships faced by the pioneers as they made their way across this vast continent in search of a better life.

Most of Utah seems to be turned over to exploiting its history or religion. The most fascinating part however is in the south boarding the State of Arizona. I'm referring to the amazing State Park of Bryces Canyon. Here nature has carved an incredible array of sculptures out of the rock creating an enormous orange natural amphitheatre created by erosion. It was named for Ebenezer Bryce, an early Mormon settler, who declared it was 'a hell of a place to lose a cow', thus failing to see the obvious beauty of the place.

11. SIN CITY

Once upon a time, there lived an evil Mafia gangster named Bugsy Siegel who was commanded by the Devil himself to build a gambling trap to lure sinners into his lair.

'Where shall I build it?' inquired Bugsy.

'Why, in my place of course', spoke the Devil, 'I believe you call it Nevada.'

It's not hard to see Nevada in summer as being Hell itself with the heat hitting 50 degrees Celsius in the shade and the hot wind dry enough to peel the skin off your face.

And so it came to be that Las Vegas was built.

God and the Devil don't get on too well and He saw that it was bad and had Bugsy shot. Not being able to smite the entire Mafia in one sitting, He then arranged for air conditioning and entertainment not of the gambling or vice nature to balance things out. He commanded Elvis to sing there seven nights a week and a host of other talented, beautiful people to perform and so Las Vegas shows came to be.

People flocked from around the world to see Elvis, the wonderful shows and the beautiful, talented people. The sinners came too for the gambling and loose woman and so today, God and the Devil battle it out for souls in Las Vegas in an eternal struggle of good versus evil, illuminated by the best light show on Earth and available to all to witness for the cost a cheap airline ticket.

The battle is a noisy one with the drone of planes bringing in the hordes, endless traffic, loud music emanating from every quarter, the jingle of slots and the calls of the street hawkers selling show tickets or pimps selling loose women. The hordes themselves wander the streets aimlessly staring in wonder at the over-the-top buildings vying with each other to be the most outlandish, bizarre or brightest monstrosity on The Strip. Inside the buildings the noise increases with the nerve-racking jangling of poker machines calling to sinners to try their luck, endless tables of card and dice games and over-the-top waiters/entertainers trying to outdo each other for the punter's favor.

Not being sinners of that kind, we were happy to see the shows and keep the Devil away from our wallets. God did a pretty good job of lightening our wallets though with the prices for the show tickets reaching into the hundreds. But He gave good value for money for He did deliver unto us Tom Jones, Cirque du Soleil, and host of other fine entertainers who gave their all in tight, slickly produced shows that had the audiences on their feet in rapt appreciation.

Sadly Elvis has gone, but he can still been seen looking and sounding a bit like someone else almost everywhere in Las Vegas. One casino even offers Big Elvis every Friday night.

Well done God!

Arriving in Las Vegas in an RV presents one or two issues not suffered by lesser motorists. The main one being that car parking buildings will not accommodate them. So they must park in one of the few areas reserved for over-sized vehicles. This is presumably to keep things nice and tidy in the car park and the big ugly RVs out of sight, an idea which should be applied to the many land whales wobbling their way between the pokies or cruising the aisles on groaning mobility scooters designed to carry cute and loveable old folk with their bobbing heads on one side and legs that have given up on them through a lifetime of hard productive work, not obscene lard factories that have eaten themselves to a standstill.

Meeting my friends Philip and Barbara from New Zealand in a hotel on the strip and getting there by RV was fun. It inadvertently enabled me to see much of central Las Vegas three or four times consecutively as I circled around looking for an RV park close to the hotel. Many of the roads seem to travel through the hotels themselves and finally lead to a car park. A wrong right turn sent me careering through the main lobby, across the gambling floor and out through the pizza restaurant before spying an enormous, nearly empty lot marked 'Employees Only'.

I could sneak in there and nobody would know I thought, but Las Vegas has uniformed security guards trying to look like police at every entrance and doorway. The police themselves are dressed in menacingly black Nazi style uniforms and carry enough weapons to invade a small Central American country. They are usually found standing over Latino or black young men who are sitting in the gutter with hands handcuffed behind their backs. The police are best handled by not looking at them.

There are two types of security guards in Las Vegas.

1. Outside Guards
2. Inside Guards

Outside Guards have to stand in the searing heat in thick, dark uniforms with heavy contraptions swinging off their belts which they have trouble seeing below their large bellies. They are therefore bad tempered and bitchy and will stop you doing stuff just to ease their suffering by passing it on to you. They guard road entrances and doors.

Inside Guards try not to do anything in case they get it wrong and are relocated outside. Ask them something and they will refer you to an Outside Guard. Inside Guards guard elevator entrances, stairwells and doors that don't go anywhere.

Ramirez, the guard who stopped me sneaking into the Employee Only car park was a hybrid. He had an air-conditioned sentry box blocking the entrance and he was mightily pissed that he had to go outside in the heat to confront me. Anxious to get back to the air-conditioned comfort of his box, he let me park so long as I didn't stay more than a couple of hours. Why don't I park closer to the building I ventured eyeing up the many parking spaces closer to the cool sanctuary of the hotel lobby. You can't park there, you have to park here in the over-sized vehicle area, he admonished. And you will need to straighten your vehicle up so others can park too, he added, exercising his power despite the heat. My rear wheels were over the white line that marked the spaces. To my left were empty spaces that reached to the horizon without a vehicle in sight. I wondered how many RVs he was expecting that night but decided against testing his logic because I just wanted to be out of the heat, even though there was a rich vein of sarcasm and satire awaiting exploitation.

The long walk back to the hotel in the unbearable, stifling heat made even worse by the heat reflecting and radiating off concrete walls, made me wonder if Outside Guards aren't just a little stupid in that if they weren't, they would probably have an inside job. This therefore would make them dangerous and unpredictable since there is nothing more worrying than an overheated stupid person with the authority to call the black-shirted police.

After deciding to check into the hotel where it was pleasantly cool instead of staying in the RV, I found that it earned me the right to park there all night provided I had a ticket saying so in my window. Since my booking was made through the internet, I still needed to check in to obtain my ticket and room key. That left my night's itinerary looking like this;

1. Meet Philip and Barbara at the Mirage.
2. Have a few pre-dinner drinks.
3. Have dinner.
4. Check in and obtain a parking ticket.
5. Deliver parking ticket to the RV.
6. Stagger back through the oppressive heat to the show across the road at the Mirage by 9:30pm.

It went instead like this;

1. Met Philip and Barbara.
2. Had a few pre-dinner drinks.
3. Had dinner.
4. Left the Mirage from the wrong exit;
    a. Admired volcano exploding out front.
    b. entered hotel across street and couldn't find check-in desk.

c. found check-in desk two miles away on other side of casino.
d. discovered a long line of people waiting to check in.
e. Asked Stephanie at counter if she could call more staff in so I wouldn't miss my show.
f. Stephanie ignored me.
g. Introduced myself to the lady behind me who identified herself as Dutch but living somewhere else and explained why it would be a good idea to have more than two staff on.
h. Kind young black woman took pity on me and offered her place in queue. Hugged her.
i. Finally got an audience with Stephanie.
j. We don't have reservations with numbers like that she sniffed after I quoted my reservation number.
k. How about looking it up under my name.
l. Nobody by that name here.
m. Maybe by credit card number.
n. Nope, show me some ID
o. Took my passport out back.
p. Yelled at her to bring back passport and not take it out of room.
q. Returned my passport.
r. Noticed that her name badge advised that she worked for Harrahs.
s. Remembered that I booked in at Imperial Palace.
t. Grovelled pathetically. Apologised profusely.

- u. Stephanie triumphantly amused. Seventeen thunderous glares and two snickers from queue.
- v. Looked at watch, 9:28pm
5. Skipped Item 4.
6. Skipped Item 5.
   - a. Ran two miles through casino looking for exit. Inside Guards looked other way.
   - b. Found exit.
   - c. Exited.
   - d. Didn't recognise surroundings so ran down car park road, around corner, up ramp and into gaze of two bitchy, overheated Outside Guards stopping air-conditioned cars trying to enter car park, questioning them on where they were going, got told they were going to car park, ordering them to proceed after most of cold air had escaped.
   - e. GET OFF THE ROAD! GET OFF THE ROAD! Roared Outside Guard as I powered towards him, my legs pumping like pistons.
   - f. 'Get off the road, *please*' I corrected as I flew by.
   - g. Like a Marvel Comic super hero who had lost his cape, I emerged into busy four lane highway and stopped to get bearings.
   - h. Traffic whizzed around me as I looked for landmark I could recognise.
   - i. Found big bright one 13.4 miles in other direction as crow flies but 17.2 miles as late show-goer runs.
   - j. Answered phone.

k. Told by Philip that show has started, nobody else allowed in and they would leave ticket at desk.
l. Ran down highway towards big bright landmark.
m. Walked down highway towards big bright landmark.
n. Ran down highway towards big bright landmark.
o. Ran past handcuffed Latino and black man in gutter.
p. Suddenly saw Mirage on other side of road!
q. Dodged, danced, ducked, dived, swerved, pirouetted and leapt through four lanes of cars trying to kill me.
r. Made median strip.
s. Dodged, danced, ducked, dived, swerved, pirouetted and leapt through four lanes of cars trying to kill me from other direction.
t. Ran down footpath knocking tourists aside who didn't have show to go to.
u. Shots from Outside Guards missed but took out two German tourists, three street lamps and an illegal immigrant pimping loose women.
v. Ran through Mirage Casino. Gamblers dived for cover under craps table.
w. Inside Guards looked other way.
x. Arrived at counter at full speed with arms out like Marathon winner.
y. Startled girl behind counter peed herself and called for Inside Guards who promptly vanished.

z. I showed my ID, she quickly gave me ticket and made a bolt for the door (engineer's joke)
aa. Doorman stepped back in horror at sight of panting, sweaty, dishevelled middle aged man staggering towards him.
bb. I snarled, flashed ticket in his direction and disappeared into darkness of arena before he could think about enforcing 'Nobody In After Show Has Started' rule and anyway, he thought, they don't pay me nearly enough to confront madmen like that, and where the hell are Inside Guards when you need them.
cc. Flashlight lady took me up 54 flights of really steep, narrow stairs and showed me my seat at far end of row.
dd. 113 people squeezed themselves up to make way for me. Excuse me. Excuse me. Thank you. Pardon. I'm sorry. Don't touch me there. Excuse me.
ee. One Land Whale at the end either refused to, or couldn't move possibly due to being wedged fatally in his seat by his fat arse.
ff. I squeezed past him. His flesh felt like clammy whale blubber.
gg. I was revolted.
hh. Settled into my seat and explained my adventure to my friends.
ii. Land Whale told me to shut up.

Returning to the correct hotel after the show and succeeding in checking in without further drama, I was awarded the coveted ticket for the car park. Arriving at the car park at the stroke of midnight, I was relieved to see that the RV was still there.

Ramirez had been replaced by Rodriguez who eagerly advanced on me from his sentry box and issued the standard 'who goes there' type challenge. It had obviously been a quiet night and he was keen to be seen by any superior silly enough to be watching at that hour, doing a splendid job so he might be promoted inside.

Since it had cooled down somewhat, I felt the urge to enter into verbal combat with Rodriguez just because it pleased me to do so.

'It's me', I responded, 'do you have the stuff?' He stopped dead in his tracks and reached for his flashlight. 'No light you fool,' I hissed! 'Give me your gun, quick!'

'I don't have a gun,' he sobbed, 'I only guard an empty car park.'

'Then where's the money,' I demanded?

'My cousin took it,' he wailed.

'You mean I can't park my RV overnight because you sold my ticket to your cousin?'

'Wh..What? Which one is your RV,' he asked bewildered.

'That one,' I pointed. He followed me suspiciously to the RV and waited in the shadows while I unlocked the door.

I deposited the ticket in the front window and relocked the door. 'Don't tell your cousin I was here tonight,' I whispered, pressing a dollar note into his hand.

I gave him a knowing wink and set off once again for the hotel.

Rodriguez watched me for a long time before retreating to the sanity of his sentry box.

It was 3am. The biggest and tallest Inside Guard anyone has ever seen was guarding the closed and bolted floor to ceiling gates to the Forum Shops at Caesar's Palace.

'That's a big unit,' commented my friend.

'My friend says you're a big unit,' I informed the goliath. He looked down at me from a great height and said,

'Excuse me Sir?'

'We wanted to go to the Forum shops,' I explained.

'They be closed,' he noted unnecessarily.

'Is it your job to see that nobody gets through here?' I queried.

'Pretty much,' he agreed.

'I see you don't have a gun,' I noted, glancing down at his belt, 'so how will you stop us if we decide to go anyway?'

'I got handcuffs,' he said smugly.

'Do they have little pink fluffy covers on them and is there spanking involved?' I inquired.

'Actually I'm a probation guard and I don't have my handcuffs yet,' he confessed, showing us his empty handcuff holder.

'Do you have to go to handcuffing school and get a diploma before they will give them to you?'

'Something like that,' he admitted.

'So if you've got no gun and no handcuffs, how will you stop us going to the Forum Shops,' I challenged?

'I'll call for back up!' he exclaimed with delight and a big smile, showing us his radio mic, the only piece of security equipment he was allowed to carry as a probationary Inside Guard.

'That's a plastic toy made in China,' I accused which gave him what could have been his first chance to use his radio in combat as he clicked the transmit button but refrained from calling for back up. I wasn't sure if he was warning us or boasting. The returning crackle and voice traffic confirmed his radio was real. We surrendered.

That the Forum Shops were securely locked and he was big enough to pick both of us up at the same time without the need for a gun, handcuffs or back up, offered conclusive proof that Inside Guards are really just pussies. I have to assume the back up if it were to be effective, would have to be Outside Guards who would no doubt be very pleased to get inside for a while. We shook his hand and left him to his job of guarding an impenetrable entrance.

In the next Casino we stumbled upon Brunhilda the Uber Guard. She was viciously armed with a gun, a taser, a club, pepper spray, radio, direct line to the President and tactical nuclear device. This armory bristled off her short squat frame giving her the appearance of a ferocious miniature Panzer tank with lipstick.

'Is that gun real?' I inquired, seeking more writing material. She looked up at me with obvious distaste, kneed me in the balls and told me to fuck off. At least that's what she obviously wanted to do judging from the look I got. In fact she turned her back and waddled off with her armory clanking and the crowd parting to let her through. I was unsure whether this was an example of a third species of Guard not previously seen, a horrifying mutation of Inside Guard or a rogue Outside Guard that had got loose and wandered inside.

I wasn't keen to find out.

An hour later in yet another casino I was sitting at the bar enjoying a quiet drink when I felt a tap on my shoulder. Each position at the bar held an embedded TV screen masquerading as a poker machine which you could play while you waited for service. Being mean, I had tried to entertain myself pressing random buttons without putting in any money and watch the screen change in the hope that maybe some drunk fool had left the bar with some credits unplayed or a program bug had opened the opportunity for a massive payout. This returned the same satisfaction as if I had put actual money in it, that is to say, none at all.

I swiveled towards the tap on my shoulder to see a man who turned out to be from Galway in Ireland and therefore completely incapable of speaking understandable English.

'Watwudyadoere?' He uttered incomprehensibly.

'What?' I asked, confused.

'What would you do here?' He repeated pointing at the screen in front him. I looked at the screen to see that he was in the middle of a game and it was showing ten of hearts, queen of hearts, king of hearts, ace of hearts and two of hearts. I did a double take and realized he had a flush in hearts but was one jack of hearts away from the perfect poker hand, a Royal Flush in Hearts and he had one more spin available. He could take the flush or risk losing it trying for the Royal Flush with his last spin.

'Wait a moment mate,' I advised, 'we shall consult Joe the bartender.' Joe, being a barman surrounded by these machines, was an obvious expert in such matters I concluded. He had been handsomely tipped an hour earlier and was as a result, in my mind at least, my groveling slave.

'Get over here Joe,' I demanded rudely in the vernacular of a New York gangster who had just tipped a barman handsomely and therefore owned his ass at least until that round of drinks was finished and needed to feel manly and in control.

Joe, who was a New Yorker and used to such shit, groveled over to us in the manner of a barman hoping for another big tip from idiot foreigners who had little idea on how or how much to actually tip and who had probably tipped too much already.

'Holy crap!' He exclaimed as he took in the picture on the screen. 'Are you serious? He'll get like, $2 for a flush and $1,000 for a Royal Flush in Hearts. Ya gotta go for it,' he ordered before turning on his heel and going back to his business as if we were a couple of idiots and with our tips, in his opinion, now spent.

'We're goin' for it I think,' I yelled to his back as if we weren't a couple idiots who had tipped too much at the beginning and had just blown the lot by demonstrating our lack of knowledge of things Vegas.

Irishman pressed the button. I imagined a drum roll in my head and everything suddenly went in slow motion as the number rolled over. The sound dimmed in the background and I'm sure the security cameras overhead zoomed in to catch the concentration on our faces and the beads of sweat forming on Irish's brow. Heads turned in slow motion throughout the Casino to watch the drama unfolding before their very eyes and all gambling came to a halt except for a lonely ball spinning slowly around a roulette wheel. *(Editor's comment: is all this necessary?)* Entranced for an eternity, we watched it click over to ... The ten of diamonds.

'Wow!' I exclaimed, 'you got a pair of tens. How much did you win?'

Studying the screen carefully, he announced;

'Five cents.'

'How much is that in Irish money?' I asked hopefully.

'Four fifths of five eighths fuck all with a hole in it.' he replied philosophically.

Irish people are obviously used to disappointing results like that and my new friend was no exception. He shrugged with resignation and ordered another drink while the Casino let out a collective sigh and returned to its frenetic activity.

'Gidday,' greeted our friends the Aussies Lex and Sharron as we pulled up the RV outside the Las Vegas house they had just bought the day before. 'We got one big enough to store your RV.' Lex exclaimed generously. I had previously asked Lex if the house he and his wife Sharron was buying had room in the back yard to for my RV. I eyed the gap in the wall that the RV was supposed to go through. Lex was optimistic but I thought there was less chance of the RV getting through there than there was of my winning the big jackpot at downtown Las Vegas or getting plucked out of the audience to stand in for Neil Diamond when he suddenly developed laryngitis on stage and needed a back up. Optimistically though, I always carry my microphone with me to the shows, just in case. ('Is there a Neil Diamond impersonator in the audience?')

Neil Diamond was in no danger that night of relinquishing the stage to me as it became clear that the RV was not going to fit.

Unperturbed Lex announced that he would have the gap widened in the morning.

The Mexican who came to look at the job wanted $600.

'Yer off ya rocka,' scolded Lex, 'I'll knock the bugga down with me bare hands before I'll pay ya that much bloody money.'

The Mexican slunk away and other options were considered instead of Lex's bare hands although I thought briefly about charging up the battery on the video camera and standing by for another sure-hit You Tube Moment.

None of us knew there was such a thing as a concrete chainsaw or that you could hire one and it could go through a six foot concrete wall like a hot knife through butter, so the chap down at the hire center claimed.

The trepidation was now mine as I fired it up.

'You can't even cut yourself on this,' the salesman had claimed. 'You can put your hand on it while it's going and nothing will happen.'

'You can put your hand on it if you like' I thought, 'mine's staying on the end of my arm.' I brought the chainsaw down on the wall and true to the salesman's description; it cut through the concrete pretty quickly. A column of concrete detached from the wall stood proudly like a statue until I gave it a kick. It fell over beside the wall and there it remains to this day since it weighs as much as the RV but has no wheels.

On the return visit a few days later, I edged the RV through the now adequate gap. Lex had plastered the cut, filled in the holes and painted it the same color as the rest of the wall. It looked magnificent. I'm sure I felt a small bump as I edged the RV inside. Proudly inspecting the now correctly parked

RV inside the compound I noticed an additional piece of concrete on the ground that I was sure hadn't been there before. The top half of the wall was now lying on the ground beside the immoveable concrete pillar. A small mark on the awning support of the RV showed where it had been clipped on the way in. 'Oops!' I thought guiltily, 'I wonder if I can get that back up, plastered down and painted before Lex and Sharron come back.' The block of concrete was as heavy as a Sherman tank and there was no way it was going back up there without a 40 foot crane to lift it.

Checking the storage areas of the RV, I discovered that I did not have a 40 foot crane and there was none in Lex's shed either.

I had just one option: Flee. Which I did.

Returning to face the music later, Lex wanted to know if I had seen the wall. Mostly, I replied not sure if he was referring to his magnificent job of plastering and painting the cut or the new demolition job I had completed earlier.

'We must have had a bloody gale force wind last night, she's knocked the top off the wall mate!'

'Crikey!' I rejoined slipping briefly into Strine (Australian accent), 'you sure it wasn't something else?'

'Can't think of anything else that could've done it,' he mused.

'I might've brushed very lightly against it with the RV,' I confessed. 'Then there might have been a small gust of wind. Or small earthquake.'

They both looked at me and Lex threw his head back and laughed.

'It actually doesn't look too bad like that,' he said to my relief.

'It actually looks better than before,' exclaimed Sharron and I made a mental note to nominate them for the Australian and New Zealand Diplomatic Mission to the UN. They could probably sort out the Middle East situation by lunch time.

'You want how much?' I repeated incredulously? 'Fifteen dollars,' the bored official behind the counter at the KOA Campground attached to Circus Circus, one the oldest and smelliest casinos on The Strip, repeated.

'Fifteen dollars to dump the contents of my septic tank down a hole in the ground that leads directly to the Las Vegas sewer system that can't count the amount of crap you send down it anyway,' I rejoined?

'Tell someone who cares,' he intoned 'or go somewhere else.'

'There is nowhere else,' I complained. 'You've driven all the campgrounds out of business with your cheap hotel rates. It cost me less to buy the crap food you have for sale at your casino than it does to get rid of it again. And I have to add that I think I have improved it,' I insulted. He rolled his bored and uncaring eyes at me and looked: piss off.

'Why don't I just pull up to one of your empty RV sites and just make my donation down the poop hole there? You look too damned lazy to get out of your seat to do anything about it and I'll be gone before an idea on how to handle it forms in your tiny, regimented, bureaucratic brain,' I said silently.

'Outside guard will see you and fire a warning shot through your head,' he replied in my mind.

'OK, the desert on the outside of town gets it,' I thought cheaply.

Emptying the contents of a week's worth of bowel movements in the desert from the holding tank of an RV sounds like an easy task, but it's a little like doing number two's in front of everyone. You're not sure who might be watching and anyway those convenient little holes everywhere in the desert are actually homes for cute little prairie dogs.

'OK then, how about a bulldozed, abandoned sub-division with no prairie dogs?' I asked myself.

'There are houses close by and someone might see you and call an Outside Guard,' I replied warily. 'They look deserted, maybe they're abandoned too?' I hoped. 'Maybe they're just at work?' I countered. 'Excellent! Then they won't know a bloody thing either way will they?'

Driving over the dusty, bone dry, sterile ground that is the base of the Las Vegas desert, to a relatively flat area with the poop side of the RV away from the nearby deserted houses, I pulled the lever and out gushed the disintegrated results of a week of bohemian living.

Slurp, said the desert as the issue disappeared almost immediately like water into a sponge and a small flower popped up in gratitude from the middle of the damp patch.

'You're welcome' I said, overcome with the warm fuzzy feeling you get when you do something good for the environment and it doesn't cost you anything.

'Am I in your way man?' I addressed the uber cool black guy in the bright red jacket, fedora hat and dark glasses.

'No man, ah can see jus' fahne.'

We were in the audience awaiting the arrival of Tom Jones to the theatre at Harrah's Casino on The Strip and he was seated slightly behind me.

'Can ya'll see anything through them dark glasses?' I teased.

'Hey man Ahm cool,' he reckoned. He swayed to and fro as only a cool dude can and I felt that pang of jealousy and impotence that one feels when one is exposed to someone so ... um, er, ah (can we delete this bit?) *Editors Note: No way!*

'What's yo gig?' I suaved impotently, trying to catch some element of cool from him.

'Mah name is Hollywood an' ah am a stah,' he announced with a flourish, handing me his bidness card which indeed did identify hisseff as *'Hollywood da Man and his Fancy Band.'*

'How come yo ass is heah and not playing no Vegas gig?' I demanded faux coolly.

'Ahm havin' me sum reeelaxation. Come to see mah man Taahm Jones do his stuuff.'

There was simply no answer to any of this and I admitted defeat having been thoroughly out-cooled. I made a mental note to investigate red jackets and how to see through sunglasses inside at night when I got back.

Our table was placed 90 degrees from the stage and had six seats. There were four of us. If we had got there early, we would have had the first four, but no, it would only takes us half an hour to drive the ten miles to the Strip, five minutes to park and five minutes to walk to the theatre so we should allow forty minutes to get the best seats. In fact it took half an hour to drive the ten miles to The Strip, five minutes to park, five minutes to walk to the entrance to the casino and three days to walk through the enormous casino to the theatre.

By the time we had reached the theatre there was a man and his wife, who was close to breaching the legal definition for Land Whale, occupying the two front seats with unimpeded views of the stage while we had to find a visual corridor past the fat heads so we too could see. Silently cursing ourselves for once again underestimating the time it takes to get anywhere in Las Vegas, we settled in for the show.

Tom Jones was extremely inconsiderate in that he moved continuously across the stage forcing us to sway back and forth so we could see around the fat heads in front of us.

Lex had the worst of it since the Land Whale in front of him was gettin' down in her seat and because she had no sense of rhythm, simply oscillated randomly in front of Lex. As the fat head with big hair waved back and forth in an irregular pattern, she created an impenetrable shield that protected Tom Jones totally from Lex's sight no matter where he moved his head. Oscillating in an opposing pattern so he could see most of time was impossible as her movements were totally unpredictable. Luckily Lex had seen Tom Jones 45 years earlier so it didn't matter so much.

'That was great,' exclaimed the Land Whale at the end of the show.

'What did he look like?' asked Lex.

Nevada is not just the home of Las Vegas of course, it also boasts the magnificent Grand Canyon for which words to describe it are hopelessly inadequate. The sheer scale of it defies belief and the sheer idiocy of some of the visitors likewise.

While it's possible to creep close enough to the edge to cast a nervous glance over the safety rail, it is also possible to climb over these sensible barriers and go where only fools and squirrels dare.

My telephoto lens captured a young man who turned out to be Australian (no surprises there!) standing on the edge of a vertical precipice some 3,000 feet above the canyon floor. A moment earlier and I would have got him standing right on the edge with his arms out looking for all intents and purposes that he was about to dive off. It was enough to give anyone standing safely behind the barriers nightmares as gusts of wind are known to blow suddenly from below.

Rural life in and around the canyon is as unlike Las Vegas life as it is possible to be.

In what seems to be a nod in the direction of Las Vegas' mobster past though, some gas stations sell not only gas and diesel but lotto, ammo, guns and beer. There's at least one car in the state that boasts to being 'dangerous' as the photo on the next page shows. What the owner might have been buying sends a shudder up my spine. Now that's a mix I would not like to run into on Saturday night.

12. CALIFORNIA DREAMING

I knew we had crossed the border into California when the overheard conversations were littered with the word 'like' in every sentence.

While this is a common enough misuse of the word in young people around the English speaking world, Californians, who were first to hijack the word and are notorious for their misuse of the English language, have raised its use to a new low.

As further evidence that they hold the rest of America in contempt, (they are as yet, like, completely unaware of a world outside the United States) they elected as Governor a man whose command of English is almost as good as his acting skills. They also coined the word *'Governator'*.

It is almost impossible to satirize a people who can say, in the course of a normal daily conversation, 'I'm like, wow! You are like, totally out there, and he was like, 'huh, are you like, serious?'"

With Hollywood being the leading influence in California, it's not surprising then that Californians lead the world in inventing bizarre new behaviors and ways of talking.

Crossing into California from Nevada is a less than riveting experience and I was disappointed not to see a sign which announced; *'You are like, entering California. Wow!'*

The area between Las Vegas and Los Angeles is essentially a desert where temperatures can reach 50 Celsius in the shade

– if you can find any. Needless to say, this is a decidedly less than advantageous place for your RV to break down.

Murphy's Law says that if your RV is to break down in the Mojave Dessert in the middle of summer and during the hottest part of the day, it will do so equidistant from help at either end. That is, 125 miles from nowhere in any direction.

'It's losing power!' my wife, who was driving, exclaimed.

'What is?' I asked.

'The engine. I can't make it go any faster than 30 miles an hour.'

'Pull over, I'll take a look.'

Once stopped, it became clear that we had a major electrical problem. The alternator had stopped charging and the battery was so flat it could no longer run the sparking plugs. The engine died and that was it. No sign electrical life anywhere in the RV's systems.

Fortunately the RV had two further batteries which were used for the house systems. If only I could link them up somehow, we could drive to the next city before they too went flat.

Tools in hand, I bravely went outside. Holy mackerel! A wave of hot air assailed me as I stepped outside. I had never experienced heat like it in my life! With heat radiating off the road and a hot wind blasting me, it was so hot I had to use a cloth to open the engine cover.

What followed was an ingenious (in my opinion at least)

rewiring of the main cables to patch one of the good batteries into the main circuitry. With every part of the engine bay and grill too hot to touch without receiving a scalding burn, this was a tricky operation made harder by the constant buffeting from passing traffic, especially the 18 wheelers which seemed to skim past at 60 miles per hour just inches from where I was working. Using all the padding I could find in the RV in way of towels and mats to protect myself from the hot surfaces, I began the operation, hoping that the cheap Home Depot tool kit I had bought at the start of the trip was up to the task and that vital nuts and bolts were not seized in place from rust. With no spare parts to make any repairs, things had to go perfectly. An RV that had been sitting for the better part of a decade doing nothing could have developed corrosion points in connections that needed to be loosened and retightened. This was no time for a faint heart.

At the back of my mind I was cautiously working on an alternative plan to save us from certain death in the desert if my repair work was to fail. With no cell phone coverage in the area, I would have to throw myself on the mercy of passing traffic. Of course everyone knows that California is populated by psychopaths and crazies who cruise these parched, unforgiving highways searching for victims whose vehicles have broken down, invite them to their lair promising salvation and then do unspeakable things to them over an extended period of time involving equipment normally used by a coroner or dentist or both, usually in dark, damp basements or deserted ghost towns from which there is no escape unless you can somehow bust out by jimmying a loose lock with a rusty nail while he's in town getting supplies. But then you would have to stagger through the desert without water or shade, avoiding the rattlesnakes and scorpions until you reached a highway where you could flag down a passing motorist. Of course everyone knows that California is populated by ...

I know all this because it's in the movies. I would have to be very careful about who I choose to stop. But what kind of vehicle does a psychopath drive? Probably not an 18 wheeler but then, they stop for nobody anyway. No time to spare. Ordinary people too are unlikely to stop since they too know that psychopaths often catch their victims by faking a roadside breakdown. Ergo, the only one who would stop to help us would be the feared psychopath himself. I had no choice. I had to succeed. Despite the heat, a cold sweat broke out on my brow and my hands trembled at the thought of a bolt breaking or a nut burring as I worked feverishly in the oppressive heat.

One by one, the bolts came undone smoothly. So far so good.

But I knew that Murphy's Law would kick in sooner or later. There is always one nut or bolt that refuses to move or will break. The tension built as I worked through the bolts that needed to be removed.

I reached the last nut and bolt. None had given me any trouble yet. If it was to happen, this would be the one. I paused, took a deep breath and started on it.

After a tense moment's resistance, it gave way smoothly. Thank God! The psychopaths would be frustrated today.

As I unwound the nut I was suddenly struck by a horrific

thought. What if I dropped the nut and it fell into the engine where I couldn't reach it?

With trembling hands, I slowly removed the last nut. Just as it came off the bolt an 18 wheeler hurtled past buffeting the RV which lurched alarmingly causing me to drop the nut and giving me a third degree burn against the red hot exhaust manifold at the same time. OMG!

Desperately I peered into the bowels of the engine bay seeking the lost nut. It had to be here somewhere I reasoned. Surely it can't end like this!

Luck was on my side this time, but Murphy had not finished with me yet.

The nut had fallen right through the engine bay onto the road, but Murphy states that when that happens, it will roll to the exact geometric center beneath the vehicle forcing you to crawl underneath to retrieve it, which is exactly where it ended up.

By this time of course, I knew that every snake and scorpion in the area had taken shelter from the burning sun under the RV and I would have to crawl the gauntlet to retrieve my nut.

On this occasion, the snakes and scorpions either were too hot and tired to bother with me or they weren't there at all and I was able to get under and out without incident.

The rest of job went smoothly and with the new battery in place, the engine fired up with a satisfying roar and we were once again on our way.

Of course with the alternator not working this battery would be depleted as well in time so all electrical equipment not needed to run the motor had to be switched off. This included the fan for the air conditioning. This was not going to be a comfortable journey.

Even with the windows down, the 50 degree Celsius heat blasted through like an oven leaving me to wonder briefly if the dungeon of the psychopath might be a cooler alternative.

Watching the gauges it became clear that we would not reach safety without another change of battery. Luckily we still had one more to call on and it wasn't long before the engine once again began to lose power and stuttered to a dead halt. With half the distance to safety covered, it would be a close run thing.

By this time we were high in the Sierra Nevada Mountains where the temperature had dropped to a more comfortable level.

Once again out came the tools but this time, the transfer was made quickly and without incident. Several psychopaths slowed down to check us out but I was able to wave them on confident that they would not be needed today.

On we rolled towards San Bernardino where we knew there was a garage that could repair the RV.

As we approached civilization at last, the engine once again began to lose power indicating that our last battery was nearly depleted.

Pulling into the garage at last, we were directed to a parking place where we could plug into mains power and finally run.

all of our systems once again and recharge the batteries. In an Apollo 13-style drama, the engine spluttered and died just as the RV was positioned in place, proving that Murphy doesn't always get his way.

13. WEDDING, THE SECOND

The reason we had travelled to the United States in the first place was not just to realize a long-held dream, but to attend the weddings of two sons of long time friends. The first was held in Wisconsin three weeks earlier. The second, for their eldest son, was to be held in San Diego.

While the first wedding was a very formal affair, the second was to be far more relaxed and informal in a typical Californian-type manner.

We arrived in San Diego the day before the wedding to be greeted by blue skies, gentle sea breezes and a perfect temperature of around 25 Celsius. What a relief! It felt like Paradise after so many weeks of oppressively hot temperatures. At last we could have the windows open to savor the cool, fresh sea air wafting through.

We were keen to lay eyes on the Pacific Ocean and dip our toes in the waters shared by our home shores in New Zealand albeit across several thousand miles of open ocean.

We had travelled 12,000 miles (20,000 kilometers) and crossed 25 states. We had touched the waters of the Atlantic, travelled from the tip of Florida to the Canadian border and now across the great western plains to the south west tip of this vast nation. We had seen an experienced much yet there was so much we didn't and couldn't see such is the size of this land.

However the pleasures of San Diego awaited us.

Like the first wedding, the second was run over three days as well beginning on the Friday afternoon at Magee Park in Carlsbad in the north of San Diego. The informal gathering was a chance to meet up with our friends once again along with a few who had attended the first wedding and travelled across for this occasion as well. It was also the opportunity to meet a new group of friends and a new family.

The ceremony itself was held at the Leo Carrillo Ranch, once the private estate of a fellow of the same name and now owned by the city.

It's been well preserved as an Old California-style working rancho and was a perfect setting for what turned out to be a perfect wedding.

As is usual in southern California, the sun shone brilliantly all day without a cloud in the sky and all activities including the reception meal and dance afterwards were held outside complete with a stunning eight-piece Mariachi Band.

Once again I was impressed by the quality of the young people and the organization of the day. The only hiccup appeared to be when the local cat got itself inserted into a dessert bowl full of cake and cream while nobody was looking.

'What are you drinking?' inquired the youngish looking man who said he was a retired brain surgeon now writing a book on brain surgery.

'The standard fare,' I replied, "Whatever's free from the bar.'

He and his wife had been at the first wedding and had made the trip especially for this one. Being retired obviously meant he had the time to do such a thing and was keenly interested in talking to me as I was the one who had travelled the furthest to be at the wedding, some 15,000 miles beating the group from England who thought the prize was theirs.

'What's your book about?' I asked politely.

'Brain surgery,' he said.

'A technical treatise for the trade or an expose for the general public?'

'Just a book about my time as a brain surgeon.' He was still trying to find the Meaning Of Life and had apparently not found it inside the heads of his patients over the years so was writing a book to see if that would scratch his itch. Apparently brain surgery had taken up all his time so there wasn't a lot left to write about and retirement was obviously not suiting him.

It could catch on, these books about surgery. Perhaps his colleagues will be inspired to write about their experiences as say, an ear, nose and throat specialist or a proctologist.

I've never quite understood the reason why there are proctologists. Oh I know they perform a very valuable service and save many lives and one has looked up my ass, but who actually aspires to be one?

There are two possibilities:

1. 'What do you hope to be someday son?'

'I want to be a proctologist when I graduate dad. I want to spend the next 30 years of my working life looking up other people's bums.'

2. 'You failed your medical exams son, there's no chance now of being a heart surgeon or brain surgeon. Best you can hope for is proctologist.'

Being a travel writer may not be as lucrative but the views are better.

The day following the wedding was an informal BBQ held at yet another park in San Diego which proved to be difficult to find in the extreme given San Diego's incomprehensible one-way traffic system which must have been set up during World War Two to confuse any enemy unlucky enough to invade and give the locals who seem to know their way around time to organize the counter attack, or so it seemed.

The park could be seen on our map, occasionally glimpsed through the trees or across from a freeway but appeared to have no roads actually connecting to it. We circled the general area 37 times before finally stumbling upon it by accident. Although at first we didn't recognize this important detail due to the fact that the park was blessed with a sign giving it a different name to the one on the map or the one we were told of the day before. Recognizing a couple of people in the general mêlée of Sunday picnickers, we realized our error once we had passed the park and then caused a major traffic snarl-up turning the RV around in a one lane road. San Diegans proved to be as adept as Floridians and New Yorkers at road-side compliments once sufficiently motivated.

However we eventually prevailed and a convenient park suddenly appeared as we approached. Unfortunately for the RV, the kerb was a little too generous and the metal step from the side door was hooked up on it accompanied by a great crunching sound. Inspection revealed that it would have to be removed before we could proceed which involved me crawling under the vehicle and attempting to kick it loose. Such photo opportunities are apparently rare in San Diego as a small but appreciative crowd gathered to watch and record me lying in the gutter beneath the RV kicking, grunting and swearing. To applause, I finally emerged, covered in road filth, oil and dust with a twisted lump of now useless metal in my hand. One wag wanted to know what steps I would now take to enter and exit the vehicle.

14. DANCES WITH SHARKS

As part of the San Diego wedding weekend, we were invited to a canoeing expedition out from La Jolla Beach, an area noted for its abundant sea life.

This was an activity that we were really looking forward to after weeks of temperatures around 100 degrees Fahrenheit (40°C).

With the temperature a balmy 77°F (25°C) and the sea temperature around the same, we were soon kitted out in life vests, little plastic whistles in case we got lost amongst the other three million people trying to sunbathe on the beach, and two-person canoes. Only one of us had any experience in paddling such vessels and then not so much in two-person craft, so the launch in through the surf with me in the front and the wife in the rear provided the watching millions with some comic relief to add to the wonderful day at the beach they were enjoying.

With the canoe buckling and twisting under a concerted assault by massive 18 inch high tsunami-like waves, pounding into us relentlessly, it was inevitable, despite our great combined talents and strength, that the life vests would be given an early test.

Dumped unceremoniously into the surf and face-planted into the sand while the canoe headed off on its own accord back to shore, we thrashed around for some seconds before realizing it was futile trying not to get wet. Meanwhile older friends whom we imagined were less experienced in the ways of the great outdoors by virtue of the fact that they all came from great cities and we from rugged rural farmland in New Zealand, had launched their vessels without a hitch and awaited us completely dry just beyond the breaking surf, bobbing up down wearing knowing but patient looks.

Bemused onlookers helpfully returned our canoe and a large crowd gathered to witness our second attempt to become seaborne.

Muttering grimly under my breath about not making further fools of ourselves, I resolved to board the vessel in deeper water beyond the breaking surf. With the wife now sitting precariously at the front of the canoe and shouting out really helpful information concerning the imminent arrival of gigantic, unstoppable and unsurvivable waves towering almost to the upper edge of the canoe, I pushed out for the safety of the deep water.

Finally, after a superhuman effort, we were beyond the surf in the relative calm of the great Pacific Ocean almost 10 yards offshore. Standing in chest deep water, all I had to do was jump into the canoe and we would be off.

My Great Leap Forward onto the canoe was an instant success. Unfortunately my wife at the front fell out in the process.

A quick mental appraisal of the situation called for me to return to the shore for another attempt rather than strike out on my own tempting though that was.

However, before this decision could be finalized and not to be left behind, she tried in vain to regain her seat resulting in the craft flipping completely over and tossing me back in the water with her.

Attempt three was much more successful. With the help of many willing hands, we were guided out past the breakers to safety with laughter ringing in our ears.

From there on we quickly mastered the art of double canoe paddling as we weaved our way first one way then the other across the bay. Our destination was a series of caves on one side of the bay where you could see seals and all manner of fish.

A sinister looking cave in the cliffs on the far side of the bay was home to a colony of seals which had the foresight to develop a pungent, really bad smell presumably to discourage predators and tourists, we being the tourists. It worked quite well for us and as a bonus extra, allowed us to use it as an excuse not to enter the cave in our canoe as did some others. Not that we were afraid of the sea surge crashing dangerously against the rocks and throwing us to a dreadful and humiliating death by drowning, concussion or both. No, that did not enter my head as I watched my compatriots who were obviously retired Olympic athletes – why else couldn't we keep up with them – navigate their way with consummate skill through the swell and into the bowels of the cave amid the honking and applause from the seals basking at the edge on the rocks on each side.

Feeling a pang of envy that this experience was beyond our courage and ability, we watched from the safety of the sea beyond the cave entrance but continued to observe loudly enough for all to hear how smelly it all was and that was the reason we were giving it a miss.

A number of ferociously named leopard sharks had been sighted in the surf by a member of our group who excitedly related to us his close encounter with these deadly beasts. Of course everyone then wanted to take a look for themselves and I wondered at the foolhardy bravery of these seemingly fearless Americans.

Naturally the sharks were nowhere to be found by the time we got there and so we all returned to the shore where we made a grand and spectacular exit on the crest of a massive 6 inch wave that swept us straight on to the beach where we were able to step out of the canoe in triumph to the obvious but well concealed admiration of the thronging crowds pretending not to notice us. Just when I thought that part of my flirtation with death was over, we were informed that the sharks were indeed out there and just on the edge of the surf. In a moment of madness I incomprehensibly agreed to partner another male member of the group out in a canoe to see them.

This time the launch through the surf was done with daring and aplomb and saw us reaching the safety of the deep water quickly and without incident. We paddled our way to the place where the sharks had been last seen and cruised around looking for sign of them.

Suddenly there they were! A dozen or more sharks around 5 feet in length were darting through the surf about 12 inches beneath our canoe. According to my canoeing buddy they were either in a feeding frenzy or a mating frenzy. He was not sure which. That left me with the uncomfortable thought that if I fell into the water, I was either going to be eaten or mated to death. Either way the sight of these creatures darting at speed under and around our small craft was a wonder to behold. Maintaining our position at the edge of the surf was difficult and required constant effort to keep the craft pointed into the approaching waves so we didn't get flipped.

Naturally such a situation cannot continue indefinitely and of course a wave caught us at angle which unbalanced us. Fighting desperately to keep from flipping into the water and falling directly on top of the sharks, we paddled first this side then the other. The canoe bucked alarmingly from side to side and it seemed that for an instance we would go under. Then it seemed we had regained control until the next wave caught us.

In what seemed an eternity we fought first one wave then the next, then the next until the inevitable happened.

We were dumped into the water in the middle of the sharks.

It is said that your life flashes before you just before you die but I was too terrified to look back on my life and in any case it may have put me to sleep, my not having had the most exciting existence up till this point.

Abandoning the craft for whatever fate awaited it, we ran across the top of the water towards the safety of the shore with the sharks lunging at us trying to tear huge chunks of flesh from our legs.

I could feel their bodies brushing past my legs as we waded desperately through the waist-deep water.

Somehow we reached the shore unscathed and after checking to see that all limbs were in place, we joined up with the others and retold our horrifying tale.

I had already begun composing my story that would be told and retold down through the ages by my awed descendants when our intrepid leader informed me that leopard sharks had virtually no teeth and were harmless to humans. This is why the beach is never cleared when they arrive and why people wander around amidst them.

'They don't bite but they can give you a nasty suck!' he teased.

I kind of liked my version which had been developing in my mind where I had survived a terrifying, frenzied attack by giant sharks longer than the canoe and that were hell-bent on making a meal of us. Pity.

15. HOME

Air travel is not as much fun as travelling in an RV, particularly since Bin Laden forced us to take our shoes off to get on a plane. But Las Vegas to Auckland is a long way by boat.

South West Airlines had a good deal connecting me to my international flight out of Los Angeles in time. All my gear was safely packed away in one suitcase so there shouldn't be a problem with my checked baggage. So I thought.

Arriving at the check in desk, I was advised that my bag, at 52 lbs, was 2 lbs overweight – just less than a kilo. 'What's the problem with that?' I asked 'My luggage allowance is 100 lbs.' Well, apparently the people who load the luggage into the planes can only lift 50 lbs safely. Anything heavier than that might strain their backs so a limit of 50 lbs per bag is imposed.

Oh.

'But,' I was informed, 'If you pay us $50.00 extra, we will take it for you.'

Huh?

'How does paying you $50.00 save the guy's back? Is the extra money to pay for a physiotherapist after he's finished? Or perhaps you hire another person on contract to help him lift it?'

Apparently not. 'There's no reason for it, it's just our policy.'

'OK, what if I spread it over two bags?'

'No problem, you can do that. In fact we can sell you a bag for just $25.00.' Smiling clerk produces an empty soft bag from under the counter.

Not a bad up-sell idea. I wondered if he was on commission. Or perhaps he's running his own little business?

'I'll buy my own bag thank you. You realize that two bags will take up more room in the plane than one bag?'

'Yes, but we don't care.'

Now, here's the rub. The extra weight was caused by an additional piece of baggage that I hadn't counted on initially. A friend in New Zealand needed an expensive piece of electronic equipment that was cheaper in the United States than in New Zealand, so would I mind bringing it back with me? It weighed exactly 1 kg or 2.2 lbs.

I had an hour to kill before the flight so I eventually tracked down a small bag for $11.00 in a shop in the Terminal.

My New Zealand friends with whom I would meet up with in Los Angeles and with whose flight to Auckland I would join up with were leaving a half hour later than me on another airline.

So now I had two bags to worry about instead of one. I packed the expensive electronic equipment into the new bag and checked it in.

An hour later I arrived in Los Angeles, found the baggage claim area and awaited the arrival of my bags. Of course my original bag was first off the carousel and I waited for the second one to arrive.

Half an hour later the carousel was empty, there was no one left and my second bag was nowhere to be seen.

A discussion with the airline representatives followed when I was told that it would 'probably be on the next flight. That happens sometimes.' Fortunately I needed to wait for my friends to arrive and when they duly did we all waited around for another hour for the next South West flight from Las Vegas to arrive.

This time the bag was there with its expensive electronic equipment safe and secure. An image of the smiling face across the counter at the airport in Las Vegas came unbidden into my mind. Had he deliberately put my bag on the wrong flight because I didn't buy it from him?

I would never know.

The airline gave me a voucher worth $50.00 for my troubles, the same sum they wanted to charge me initially for the extra weight. I wondered when, if ever, I would have the opportunity to use it. The conflicting ironies of the situation were too much for me to consider without a quiet moment or pen and paper.

The end of a journey is always a mixed blessing. On the one hand you feel like there are more places to see, more people to meet and more things to experience if you only stayed a little longer. Yet on the other hand, you can't wait to return to the familiarity of your homeland and to see friends and family again.

It is said that travel broadens the mind but in some people it simply reinforces their prejudices. I've met a few of the latter and I hope and believe that I am in the company of the former.

I have barely scratched the surface of this vast and interesting land with its myriad of peoples. What I've learned has simply increased my appetite to learn more.

The RV stands alone in Las Vegas awaiting my return. It sits beckoning me, inviting me to take once again to the roads of the United States. To see the places I haven't seen, to meet the people I haven't met and to experience the things I am yet to experience.

One day.

CPSIA information can be obtained at www.ICGtesting.com
Printed in the USA
BVOW05s1218260214

346082BV00017B/241/P